## Vol. II
### Recovering the Woman Within
### The Love Is Over, Not You

Visionary Author
**PATRICE BUSH**

Published by Victorious You Press™

Charlotte NC, USA

Copyright © 2022 PATRICE BUSH All rights reserved.

No part of this book may be reproduced, distributed or transmitted in any form by any means, graphic, electronic, or mechanical, including photocopy, recording, taping, or by any information storage or retrieval system, without permission in writing from the author except in the case of reprints in the context of reviews, quotes, or references.

While the author has made every effort to ensure that the ideas, statistics, and information presented in this Book are accurate to the best of his/her abilities, any implications direct, derived, or perceived, should only be used at the reader's discretion. The author cannot be held responsible for any personal or commercial damage arising from communication, application, or misinterpretation of the information presented herein.

Unless otherwise indicated, scripture quotations are from the Holy Bible, King James Version. All rights reserved.

TITLE: EVOLVE II

First Printed: OCTOBER 2022

Cover Designer: NADIA MONSANO

Editor: CHARMAINE CASTILLO

ISBN: 978-1-952756-89-4

ISBN: 978-1-952756-90-0 (Ebook)

Library of Congress Control Number: 2022917992

Printed in the United States of America

For details email joan@victoriousyoupress.com
or visit us at www.victoriousyoupress.com

# TABLE OF CONTENTS

**Foreword:** ............................................................................... 1

**Evolve or Dissolve?** ............................................................ 7
Patrice Bush, Visionary Author

**My Interruption of Everything** ...................................... 25
Nichelle Nelson

**I Am Stronger Than My Fears!** ...................................... 37
Suan-Nesha Fuller Scott

**From Pain to Progress** ..................................................... 47
J. Tyneka Nelson

**Self-inflicted Drowning** ................................................... 59
Venus J. Jackson

**The Voice from the Backseat** ......................................... 73
Kerrie L. Brittingham

**I Believed He Was Everything I Wanted** ..................... 85
Dwan Warren

**No Regrets** .......................................................................... 97
Kristan Bennerman

**About The Authors** ........................................................ 109

# Foreword:

## A Rare and Precious Gem
## By Chantia Carter, MSW LCSW - Therapist

We were never formally introduced, so I can't remember "meeting" Patrice for the first time. It was more like I remember being impressed by her presence. I admired her passion for her clients and her consummate professionalism. We began our relationship as school social workers who later became what we coined as "sister-preneurs." I am a Licensed Clinical Social Worker (LCSW) who, through my private practice, Art of Peace Wellness PLLC, in Charlotte, North Carolina, has committed to a mission to provide support to healers, helpers, and heroes. I provide access to a unique array of therapeutic approaches which supports our goal of holistic and comprehensive wellness. In other words, I help healers heal.

My timeline found alignment with Patrice's timeline when we each needed to find a place to lease for our budding businesses. The idea of partnering in a shared location was mutually serendipitous. Our cooperative goal to secure a lease together came to fruition in March 2016. Our dream was manifested. Each of our individual businesses shared one office space and it was then when I quickly realized what a rare and precious gem Patrice was.

Brilliantly faceted diamonds are very rare and expensive treasures. The process used to transform pure carbon into a dazzling diamond requires the carbon deposit to undergo intense heat and unimaginable pressure. Patrice Webb-Bush is her given name, but her name is also Petite Powerhouse of Faith. Don't let the slight frame fool you; what she lacks in height, she more than makes up for in grit and tenacity. She often says, "Great things come in small packages," and she is a beautiful exemplification of the truth in that saying.

Because of her example of how to handle the intense pressures of life, I seize this moment to tell her directly, "Patrice, you are stronger than you think you are. You have power beyond your wildest imagination in your reserve, and when you need it, your innermost fortitude will not fail you. You are an unstoppable force, created to surpass the fires (the trials of this life) and come out as gold--not even smelling like smoke! Although it may not be easy, no matter what it is -- you've got this!! I know, because God is faithful, and I'm so glad you don't have to look like what you've been through!" Patrice is a manifestation of this amazing archetype of divine impartation.

I met Patrice over twelve years ago when our careers paralleled, working together as school social workers within the Charlotte Mecklenburg school district. I became curious about her entrepreneurial side when I began to hear about marriage enrichment workshops she was offering (in addition to working with the students and their families within the district).

*Foreword*

One of our many shared experiences was the reduction in workforce due to budget cuts within the school district where we both served. It is curious to me that any urban school district would ever consider discarding the student support workers through layoffs, but then again, a tiny speck of sand (the beginnings of a pearl) is a little less than an irritant to the oyster.

The school social workers who worked within our district were given two options. The first option was to resign from our position. The second option was to obtain a second master's degree in counseling and then take any vacant counseling position within our system. That ultimatum placed Patrice in a precarious position. She faced the prospect of being without her income, which would negatively impact her family financially, or going back to graduate school. That presented quite a challenge for a very pregnant mother and wife, but Patrice, the rose that grew from concrete, bravely moved forward to get that second master's degree. Patrice didn't allow the pressure and stress of that situation to crush her, and in spite of it, maybe partially because of it, she not only survived, but she thrived. By the way, the beautiful child she birthed during that difficult time period became Junior Pre-Teen Miss Carolina at the age of 11. She also became an author, public speaker, model, and a Disney actress.

Holding two master's degrees (Master of Social Work and Master of Arts in Counseling), Patrice continued to serve in her capacity to remove barriers to education by supporting students and their families challenged by homelessness. As she continued to grow in her social work and counseling skills, she founded *It*

*Takes 2 Marriage Coaching*. While providing award-winning service to couples from thirty-nine states, serving as the keynote speaker at couples' conferences, and being sought after for radio and television appearances, Patrice was carrying the pressure and stress of a very private burden.

In spite of her public success, she confided in me that she was in a situation and needed to find her way out of it because she felt trapped. When she shared with me the details, I know the weight of what she endured would have crushed the average woman. Finding purpose in what she faced and overcame, I witnessed how Patrice navigated on a journey which called for a level of vulnerability and authenticity that many steer clear of. It is so befitting that her signature color is purple because Patrice is a supernatural wonder woman, the epitome and embodiment of grace under pressure, and is worthy of her beautiful amethyst adorned cape.

Committed to doing the work necessary to fortify and heal her broken places, Patrice mastered her peace, and what a beautiful masterpiece she is. Transforming her hurt into healing, she uses that healing as a source of strength. Patrice draws from that healing strength and pours it out, not only in this project, but in her other books as well.

An amazing entrepreneur, woman, and momma of three beautiful daughters, Patrice is the gift that keeps on giving. I am very grateful that God allowed me to see the kind of power and presence that is available when someone commits and submits to the process of healing themselves. Her personal commitment to mend herself is magnified when she reaches out to help others who need to heal in similar broken places. I will forever be grateful for her journey, her testimony, and her faithfulness!

Patrice once said, "God gave me this grand mission of strengthening families. I have learned, no matter what my life circumstances look like, God expects me to fulfill His mission," and she has held true to that vision from the day we met. Processed through pain, and holding space for others to heal, Patrice is a diamond and the prototype of a healed healer. The glow of the shine of her steadfast spirit will continue to light the way for those who need it.

Who can find a virtuous woman? for her price is far above rubies. Proverbs 31:10 (KJV)

Chantia Carter, MSW, LCSW
Art of Peace Wellness PLLC, CEO
980 277 2079

"Self-care is good for the soul"

# *Evolve or Dissolve?*

## Patrice Bush, Visionary Author

*"Do not let your anger lead to hatred, as you will hurt yourself more than you would the other."* - Stephen Richards

The water in the shower was so hot and had been running for so long the steam was escaping from under the bathroom door. I sat on the bed, mindlessly watching TV while scrolling on my phone. Facebook was consuming me as it often did, because, let's be honest, we are all intrigued by the lives of others. As I was scrolling, liking, reading, and laughing, a notification popped up indicating someone had left a comment on my business' social media page. The name associated with the comment was a name I recognized.

My husband and I had been married for nine years. We had three amazingly talented and beautiful daughters, a beautiful home that my husband and I designed and we enjoyed incredible vacations multiple times a year. Our careers were solid and we were living out what I thought was the American Dream. We had the typical marriage challenges associated with two people with opposite personality traits, but they seemed to balance out. I talked a lot, was always laughing, singing, and dancing and I'm sure I just plain got on his nerves with all of my extra. I was also spoiled, a bit impatient and very extroverted. His personality was the opposite of mine. He was a guarded and extremely introverted homebody, but he always had a laid-back manner and enjoyed having a good time. Our challenges mostly involved communication issues or struggles with conflict resolution.

In addition to doing in-office counseling with couples, we were hosting successful marriage retreats all over the country. I was beefing up our social media presence by posting videos and pictures from our latest retreat from a month earlier. My husband and I had taken new professional headshots wearing our new *It Takes 2 Marriage Coaching* shirts and one of our professional pictures as a couple was well on it's way to becoming viral. With well over 10,000 likes and equally as many comments, my private practice as a marriage counselor was booming. Needless to say, whenever I receive a notification of a new comment on our business page I am eager to check out what the world thought about my baby, my brainchild, my business and ministry.

Now, back to the shower scene. I was eager to check out the comment, and when I saw it, it changed the way I viewed my marriage, my husband, and even my house.

I noticed that several people had been tagged and the comment was followed by several laughing emojis. I was a bit confused as I reread the comment several times. Then it dawned on me! I recalled reading an exchange of text messages from a person I believed to be a friend of my husband. My hands started trembling, my heart began to race, and I could feel the anger boiling on the inside of me when I realized that just ten months prior, I learned she was much more than just a friend.

I immediately left our master suite to go check on my girls. Their bedrooms were located on the opposite side of the house, but I wanted to protect them from witnessing their mother's wrath. I was relieved and thankful to find each of them sleeping soundly. As I made my way back to our bedroom, I was numb, but I was also so pissed it scared me. I walked back into the bedroom, sat down on the bed, and watched the steam continue to roll from under the bathroom door. I thought about the comment and realized the significance of the laughing emojis. She was literally laughing at me. She was laughing at me as a marriage counselor, she was laughing at me as a wife, and she was making a mockery of me.

She had tagged their colleagues, all of whom were aware of the extent of their relationship. I was the only one who was not aware. When she posted that comment on my business page, it became personal. The post went beyond her relationship with my husband because now she had included me. She wanted me to know who she was and what she thought of me. I figured if she wanted me to know about them and was bold enough to bring it to my business page, their relationship was much more serious than I realized.

With tears streaming down my face, I contemplated my next move, but I really didn't know what I would do next. I called my sister, told her what was happening, and asked her to come pick up my girls. I thought it might be in their best interest to not witness what was about to transpire in their home.

I recall storming into the bathroom, snatching back the shower curtain, and as the tears streamed down my face he repeatedly asked me, "What's wrong?" For a moment, I just stood there holding my phone, but every part of me wanted to physically attack him. When I looked at his face, my anger immediately turned to a profound sadness.

SIDEBAR: This was not his first affair. When I found out about the first affair, I hit him, which is something I regretted for months. Even in a fit of rage, there is never an excuse to put your hands on another person, ever! I had learned that lesson well, and even though my husband was clearly not giving me a better version of himself, it was only by the grace of God that I gave him a better version of Patrice.

"You promised me this would never happen again and now you have brought another bitch into our marriage!" I screamed. I screamed a lot of other things at him too, and I don't remember everything I said after that, but as I turned to leave the bathroom, I said, "You will call her and tell that bitch to never come at me or my business again. You have ruined our family! Our kids and my business are all I have left. You can never take my role as a mother, and I will be damned if you ruin the business I have built! Tell her if she ever approaches my business in any form or fashion again, she will live to regret it, and so will you!"

When I finally gave him room to speak, his only comment was "She did what? Oh, my goodness, I will call her. I will make sure she never does that again!" He continued to deny having any kind of relationship with her beyond just friendship and even though he had a concerned look on his face, his words and actions were not aligned. There was no apology, no ownership of his actions, and no fight for our marriage.

When I walked out of that bathroom, I knew our family home, which I was so proud of would never be the same. It suddenly felt like a strange and foreign place and I didn't know how or when, but I knew it was time to go.

For the next twenty-three months, fear had me stuck. I was living in turmoil and literally fighting with myself every single day. As soon as I woke up and looked in the mirror, I could hear the questions bombarding my mind:

- How could I miss the red flags? Hell, he randomly stopped wearing his wedding ring a couple of months ago and I was still giving him the benefit of the doubt.
- Why did I think he would change? This is the second woman he brought into our marriage. I stayed with him through the first affair, attended marriage counseling sessions for us and thought he would never do it again.
- Am I not attractive anymore?
- Maybe I gained too much weight after having our third child. The first affair happened when our youngest was eight months old and now she is five years old.
- He used to be so into me, what went wrong?
- What did I do to make him seek other women?

- Did I forget who I was? Did I let myself go?
- How could God forsake me? I don't deserve this!
- I've been watching him text and talk to this lady for ten months, why didn't I speak up sooner?
- He pays all the bills, so how can I leave and take care of myself financially?
- Our kids are in private school. How can I afford the tuition?
- I haven't lived alone since I was twenty two, I'm too scared to live alone! How can I move out on my own?

I didn't have an answer for any of those questions because, honestly, I didn't know the answers. I asked him quite a few questions, but he never responded with anything significant. I knew I wasn't a perfect wife, she doesn't exist, but I knew I worked very hard at being the best wife I could be. I am thankful for the understanding I now have that cheating is a choice and not a result of not cleaning enough, cooking enough, enough sex, etc.

The first twelve months that proceeded that incident felt like a recurring nightmare. I cried more than I smiled and was literally piecing together everything I had previously ignored or minimized. I was convinced he would never cheat on me again. He always made me feel, for the most part, that things were great between us. We rarely argued, neither of us kept late hours outside of the home, and he said yes to almost anything I wanted. Our last anniversary trip was a surprise trip to Vegas which I planned and paid for. It was on his bucket list, so I just knew I was going to get the wife of the year award for that trip. One month after returning home from Vegas is when I first became acquainted with the name of said "Facebook wrecker." Yep, that was my thank you.

If I were to describe how I felt, using an analogy, I would paint the following picture:

It felt as if my husband and I were sharing an inner tube and floating along enjoying the beautiful ocean around us. We were watching our kids play in the sand and feeling the blessing of God's sun. While floating, I begin to hear the sound of air escaping from the inner tube and then it begins to deflate. Suddenly, I am no longer floating along, but instead, I am in the water drowning and fighting to breathe.

That is how I felt. I was completely unprepared to be left in the middle of the ocean, alone and unable to catch my breath. Every day I was drowning and would have done anything for a breath of fresh air.

I wore a mask after that, and no matter where I was, I wore it. I wore it at work, with my family, with my friends, and even around my daughters. I was known as the strong one, or the one others could depend on when they needed a shoulder to cry on. I was a therapist who was paid to fix problems, yet I was drowning in my own. I felt alone and isolated in a crowd and felt no one would understand the marriage coach wanting to leave her marriage. I didn't think I would have any support of my decision to divorce, and felt I would be judged by everyone, including my friends and family. I was burdened with the thought that my daughters would never forgive me for leaving their dad, and for me, everything was seemingly going wrong. In that moment of despair, I recalled a powerful truth which I had held onto from my youth. I knew in my core, that when everything seems to be going wrong, God is always right, so from that moment forward, I sought God more than I had ever sought Him in my entire life.

Praying was as vital to me as eating and drinking water. Why? Because I knew if I didn't have God helping me to control my behaviors and my tongue, I would have become someone I wasn't proud of. I knew my anger would turn into hate and then revenge, turning my home into a literal hell. I would never want to subject my kids to that, so as the old folks would say, I kept myself near the cross. I listened to Christian music all the time, prayed in my head all day, kept attending church, and I read God's word even when I didn't understand it. I asked God to keep me sane and give me a strategy.

Y'all know God answers prayers, right? In a dream, He confirmed that He would give me double for my trouble and confirmed that I had been released from our marital covenant because of my husband's infidelity. God also reassured me I was still under His protection, His love, and His calling for my life. Then, just like that, my business took an unexpected turn upward! I had a waiting list of couples choosing to be counseled by me. Every marriage retreat, workshop and event I was offering was selling out! God showed me that my gift was not contingent upon who I was married to, nor was it contingent upon whether I was even married. He had given me a gift and placed a calling on my life to strengthen families through marital counseling and he did not remove that gifting or calling just because I encountered marital challenges of my own. I was feeling very much like Moses because I was second guessing everything God was calling me to be. The fourth chapter of Exodus became my favorite chapter of the Bible. God does not call the qualified, He qualifies those whom He calls. I wrote that everywhere and on everything. That's when the shift began to happen.

What was once anger shifted into fear, and that fear shifted into faith! I had faith that I would get through that battle, that my girls would be able to withstand the transition, and faith that my private practice would continue to grow. I extended my faith to believe that I would not lose my mind, and I had faith to believe I would love again.

Forgiveness, in a psychological sense, is the intentional and voluntary process by which one who initially feels victimized undergoes a change in feelings and attitude regarding a given offense and overcomes negative emotions; such as resentment and vengeance.

The next eleven months were a game changer! My strength was being renewed day by day and my incredible village held me up in ways I didn't know was possible. Most of them were not even aware of the hell I was living in, but God put me on their hearts, and they reached out and loved on me.

I was still fearful, but I was no longer afraid. Although I hadn't physically moved out of the house my husband and I shared, I had already left emotionally. Research tells us that women typically leave emotionally before they leave physically, while men tend to leave physically first and then emotionally. I was fitting the status quo. I was emotionally and sexually unattached to him. I asked God to take away the desire I had for my husband so I could do what was best for me, which was to leave. He answered my prayer.

God does not intend for any of us to be harmed physically, emotionally, or sexually. It is a myth that God forbids divorce. In the Bible, God grants permission for divorce in many situations, including adultery and cases of abuse. As my faith in God grew, the strength I needed to leave my marriage grew. My husband was unwilling to go to counseling and unwilling to own up and accept responsibility for his second affair. He was unwilling to communicate to me where our marriage fell short, or how and why the affair happened. He was simply unwilling to try, so I had to be willing to choose me!

While God was helping me to rebuild my self-esteem, my business was continuing to grow. I invested in myself through therapy and invested more time with my children. My girls and I became tight like glue. Before my great grandmother left this earth, she told our family to stick together like two hands gripping each other, and to stay so close that air couldn't get in between us. I applied that concept to the relationship I had with my daughters, and they had no idea how their love for me was literally getting me through life at that point.

The hate that I had for my husband slowly began to dissipate. I didn't ask God for help in forgiving my ex, but it just happened. You cannot be in consistent communication with God with hate in your heart. It was as if my love for God forced me to love my husband. I'm not talking about an intimate love, but the kind of love one would have for another human being. The love I had for God gradually led to forgiveness. Before it was time for my daughters and I to move out of the house, even though my heart wanted to continue to hate him, I was able to forgive. I realized the hate in my own heart towards him was making me bitter, irritable and seemingly less than caring of those close to me. My choice to forgive my ex has greatly contributed to our ability to effectively co-parent.

In regard to the women he cheated on me with, they owed me nothing. I didn't feel a need to forgive them because the marriage commitment I made was between me, my husband, and God. So many of my friends wanted to fight the women, but I was the one talking them off the ledge.

Accountability was an important component of my healing process. I am a very ambitious woman, and I had to acknowledge my part in the damage of our marriage. There were times when I may not have been very patient while I waited to see some semblance of what I considered to be growth in my husband. I encouraged him to want more from life, but my constant nudges were filled with unrealistic expectations because what I really wanted was for him to be more like me. That was an unfair expectation. After a few years of that, I sucked it up and began to look beyond his career complacency and I just assumed he was looking beyond my faults too. No matter who overlooked whose faults in the marriage, what I was not going to do was keep adding infidelity to the list of faults I overlooked. So, yes, by the time the second affair happened, there was nothing I wanted more than to let that last woman have him because it was a NO for me.

I began meeting with a therapist on a weekly basis and grew stronger emotionally. My daughters were also adjusting to the transition and before I knew it, my practice was doing so well I was in a financial position to take the final and most critical step; move out.

## Evolve or Dissolve . . . It's Your Decision

At the end of what had proven to be the most difficult twenty three months of my adult life, I packed up half of my bedroom furniture and moved to a rental home across town. My oldest daughter was moving to college, and I was literally starting my life over. I moved into our house with my two youngest daughters and within three days, I was able to furnish their new bedrooms. My sister decorated our bathrooms, and my mom helped with furnishing the loft. Within the next month, I was able to furnish the living room, but while replacing our material things was important, it was more important that I fill the voids we were missing in our lives as a result of our transition. We shared moments of tears as we mourned the loss of family (in the traditional sense) and we were missing my older daughter who was away in college. The girls' father was no longer in the same house as them which added to the difficulty of the transition. We all needed time to adjust.

To ease the process of our transition, we established new traditions. Dinner time was always a special time to talk, laugh, or cry while sharing about our day. We spent many nights having sleepovers in the living room, and during the day we enjoyed riding bikes in our new neighborhood. We made plans for our future, and created memories as we traveled together. Of course I taught my daughters about entrepreneurship, because, after all, their mom is a serial entrepreneur.

My daughters started businesses that are still thriving and expanding today. I began writing books and they followed suit. We are a household of three business owners, authors, and public speakers, and a gymnast and an uber talented senior in college majoring in business who can also sing you into bliss.

## *We Have Evolved*

The devil comes to steal, kill, and destroy, but I am convinced he can only steal what is unprotected. God protected us, kept us sane, and kept us fighting; thus, the devil didn't steal my marriage. God exposed the dark and painful places in my marriage, and I made the choice to walk away and choose me. Even in my sadness, I never lost my inner joy. Even in my fear, I was never afraid. Even in my despair, all I had to do was lean into God for relief and although I felt alone, I was never lonely. Through His power, God revealed that truth and allowed me to know that He was always on the journey with me and my daughters. God, you are good, and for that, I thank you!

To evolve in this world is to be human, but to evolve into your best self when you are in the worst circumstance is supernatural.

Today, I am happy, whole, recovered, renewed, healing, and at peace. I said "healing" because healing is a process. There are times when I struggle emotionally thinking about the divorce, which signifies that I am still healing, but those moments of emotional struggle are becoming less frequent.

Since choosing myself and divorcing my marriage, my private practice has grown exponentially. *It Takes 2 Marriage Coaching* has served thousands of couples and I now have a team of therapists who serve alongside me. God continues to confirm, daily, my calling to help marriages. This book is the fourth relationship book I have written, and each of them has been an Amazon best seller. God has presented me with opportunities to make media appearances and to be recognized nationally as an award-winning therapist. I have received several book deals from major publishing companies, and I speak on several platforms about healthy relationships. I am a mom, a "Momager," and an advocate for marriage and love!

Once you've been drowned, hurt and broken, allowing yourself to become vulnerable can be a difficult task. Every day, get up, and put one foot in front of the other. There may be days when you experience moments of being impatient with love and may even push it away, but it's okay to feel that way. Healing is a process. You will eventually be doing well more days than you are not, and when that happens, you will know you are on the right track.

Those nine years of marriage changed me, but they made me better and not bitter. I look forward to one day being married again to a man who wants to be a husband and values marriage the same way that I do. God promised me double for my trouble, and I am standing on that promise. I had a choice, and I chose to evolve rather than allowing my situation to dissolve me. My heart is open to love, and I am loving again. You can also choose evolution!

**Three affirmations that helped me get through, and I hope they help you!**

1. Other people's opinions do not define me.
2. I can be strong and weak at the same time.
3. Doing what is best for me is doing what is best for others.

**Three questions I would like to ask to help you in your evolution.**

1. What fear did you once have that never materialized?
2. How long did you allow that fear to keep you from moving forward?
3. The next time you feel fear, I challenge you to "do the thing" anyway. Do you accept my challenge?

## REFLECTIONS FOR YOUR EVOLUTION

# My Interruption of Everything

## Nichelle Nelson

Well, Terri McMillan girl, I tip my hat to you because your book helped me get through the most trying time of my life. With my interruption, and in that, I found my healing.

I had printed out everything I could find to print, and with a knife in my hand, I screamed at him, "How could you treat me this way?" I threw the pictures, the love letters, the cards, and the phone records on the bed and demanded an answer. After five years of marriage and four kids (three babies who died in the womb), I came face to face with the fact that my husband had a FIANCÉ.

After a lot of screaming, cussing, and verbal assaults, he finally admitted that she was his fiancé! The only thing I remember after that was slapping the taste out of his mouth. It was a highly emotional moment that I'm not too proud of, but he was lucky that was all I did to him. That night I told him to leave and not come back if he knew what was good for him. I woke up the next morning with my head pounding, lying in bed alone, and wondering, "How did I get here?"

He did not come home that night. Thursday through Sunday, he was *supposed* to be at a conference. However, our son spotted him wiping down his truck on that Saturday. When I found out he was back and didn't bother coming home to face me, I was beside myself in anger. I fired off text message after text message to him and said a lot of awful things. I was in an awful place and wanted to hurt him as badly as he had hurt me. When he finally came home to face me, at about 10:00 p.m. that Sunday, he didn't *feel* like talking.

"Oh, HELL no! You are going to talk to me! You at least owe me that much!" I yelled. I was livid and he kept giving me the same responses.

"I F*d up. She's not really my fiancé. I just said that so you would squash the conversation."

I could not believe he was actually hoping I would squash it. I thought he must have lost his mind thinking that he could put a tramp before his wife. What kind of man does that? Isn't that in the player handbook for men that the side chick never comes before the Mrs.? Not ever!

When reality set in, I was angry and disappointed in myself. My self-confidence began to shrivel up and the thoughts rolled over and over in my mind.

"Why didn't I see it sooner?"

"Why didn't I leave him the first time he cheated?"

"Oh that's right, I stayed because he threatened to commit suicide."

Regardless of the magnitude of thoughts which flooded my mind at that point, one thing was painfully obvious to me. My marriage was over!

I thought about all the time I had invested over the years in trying to fix our marriage. It had been at least three months since he last showed up for one of our marriage counseling sessions. Before that, it had been six months. During that particular session, he told the counselor how well things were going, but I challenged his statements by exposing how little effort he was actually putting forth. I had been waiting and begging for years for more attention, affection and romance, but his effort produced not nearly enough of what I was expecting. I was tired of being at the bottom of his list of priorities and felt I should come before his career and his so-called boys. My dissatisfaction was evident as I voiced the way I felt about his continued disrespect. Out of frustration, I began to cry as I always did at that point, and he immediately shut down. I couldn't believe how childish he was at times, and I just wanted to yell at him to grow the hell up! I knew better than to marry a man who I was unequally yoked with, but I kept asking God to touch his heart, and, yes, change him. Thoughts of earlier times in our relationship flowed through my mind and as I recalled those moments, I regretted the time I allowed him back into my life. We had dated off and on again for about six years and after he had a serious car accident, I loaned him some money to get another car. He was supposed to pay me back but, after several months with no payment in sight, I went to his job and showed out just a tad. He left work to go to the ATM, brought me back my money, and said, "You know I still love you." I didn't see him again until three years later when I spotted him in a store.

I never expected to run into him again, but I saw him as I was passing an aisle. He was talking to a lady who had a child with her, so my first thought was, "He must have gotten married." I kept walking because he was the last person I wanted to see. He saw me and yelled my name. "What's up, Model?" Yes, Model was me. I looked back and saw him quickly approaching me, but I kept walking. When he finally caught up with me, he wrapped his arms around me from behind, and I started laughing.

"Get off of me before your wife starts tripping! I don't need that kind of drama," I said.

"She's not my wife, she's just an old friend I ran into. Do you have a man?"

"If I did, you just violated him! But, no, I don't have a man."

"Well, you do now, and I'm never letting you go again!"

As lame as that was, it warmed my heart and I fell for it. He was just so fine back then. He walked around the store with me, holding my hand, kissing me on the cheek, and helping me pick out toys for my son. He said he was making up for lost time when he paid for my entire purchase. Later that evening he came back to my house, helped me wrap all the presents, and we set them up under the tree. My son was not expected to return home until the following day, so we stayed up all night laughing, reminiscing, kissing and dancing. The feelings we once had for each other were rekindled and it was as though those feelings had never left and the problems we once had never even existed.

After Christmas, we became inseparable. He was always at my house, took me to meet his parents and family, and was loving me as if his life depended on it. Three months later, I found out I was pregnant.

*SIDE BAR:* Young ladies, always protect yourself! If you are going to have sex with a man, bring your own condoms. Diseases are widespread and you just don't know who you are laying down with or who they have laid down with. Protect your essence because not everyone deserves to be tied to your soul for life!

When I told him I was pregnant, he told his family immediately. They were all very excited, as I was carrying their first grandchild, niece or nephew, and the heir to their throne. My parents and family, on the other hand, were not as receptive and let their concerns be known.

"You're not married, how are you going to raise another child?"

"You haven't even known him that long!"

My rebuttal to address my family's concern was that I had actually known him for six years and even though we dated off and on in the past, we were finally deciding to settle down. I should have listened to my parents.

On Valentine's Day, he and I went to an upscale restaurant with his parents, his brother and his brother's wife. The men each presented their wives with a special gift. Well, my man had three gifts for me. He stood and gave a little speech about how he had been searching for me for the past three years, how he had never loved anyone the way he loved me, and how he had straightened up his life for me. He handed me some beautiful flowers and told me to select one of the three gifts he had for me. Two of the gifts were on the table and it was obvious that one was a gift basket and the other appeared to be a perfume box. I chose the gift he had in his hand and was hiding behind his back. I had no idea he was about to get down on one knee and propose. At the moment when he was asking me to be his wife, my best friend and her kids appeared from out of nowhere. The tears were flowing and I was so happy. I said yes!

When I was sixteen weeks pregnant, my whole world changed when I found out we were having a girl! In my mind, I had already planned her entire life. I had envisioned us dressed in matching outfits, and dreamt of her appearing in magazines, on billboard and in commercials. The name I had already picked out for her was Ariana Nyri, and dreamed about her becoming a model and having her college education paid for before she reached the age of five. She was my dream girl, my mini-me, and my very own baby doll.

My husband was out of town working and was not expected to return for another few weeks. During the time he was away, I developed a severe infection that landed me in the hospital. It was a life-or-death situation. My father was on his way to the hospital, but in the meantime, my husband's parents, his brother and sister-in-law, and my mother were there in the room with me. The doctor was explaining my condition to my husband over the phone.

"Sir, if we don't take the baby right now, we are going to lose them both" the doctor told him. It was up to my husband to make the final decision. I felt so helpless. I just laid there and cried out to God.

"Please don't let them take her from me."

I was ready and willing to give up my life so she could live.

My plea continued, "Please don't take her from me, God! Please fix it, Lord."

I begged my husband not to make the decision to take her from me, and as they rolled me out of the room, I continued to beg, "Please Lord, PLEASE!!"

With my mother by my side, Ariana Nyri came right out. At nineteen weeks and five days, she came out without a breath, or a sigh, or even a whimper. I laid there looking at my baby girl, who was already gone, and I just cried. I wouldn't let anyone take her out of the room. I needed her. We took pictures of her for her daddy, and I eventually mustered up enough courage to let them take her out of the room. I was done with God!

I was left cold and empty inside and spent the next year and a half pushing everyone away and moving through life without a purpose. I still needed to be a mom to my son, and quite frankly, if I didn't have him to love on and take care of, I would have taken my life. I'm so thankful that God held on to me, even when I walked away from him.

Several years passed before I was able to forgive my husband for his numerous affairs with multiple women. I was also angry at myself for continuing to believe in him the way that I did. Admittedly, he was my weakness. It was an extraordinarily hard task to forgive him because I hated him and believed all three of our babies were still born as his punishment for his infidelity. Our babies came into this world unable to breathe and I blamed him for that.

It took years for me to break free from him and it also took a while for me to trust myself again. I struggled to understand how I allowed his love to blind me, but at the end of the day, I see those losses as a blessing because it released me from being tied to him in any way whatsoever.

It took more than four years before I was able to even talk to a man, much less go out on a date. It took even more time to trust again. Trusting someone to love you the way you deserve to be loved takes patience and it also takes healing. Whether you've been emotionally abused, verbally abused, or physically abused, it's all abuse. When you violate someone's love, trust, heart, and their lives, you are an abuser.

Being counseled by my minister, Dr. Edward Riley of Inheritance Church of Christ, was instrumental in helping me overcome the trauma of years of abuse. I read a book by Dr. Tony

Roach called God's Love Bank that not only taught me about my old self love, but it introduced me to the journey of discovering my New Self-Love. I had to understand the "New Self-Love Core Values of Jesus", which are New Self-Honesty, New Self-Courage, New Self-Forgiveness, New Self-Power, New Self-Purpose, New Self-Excellence, New Self-Image, New Self-Discipline, New Self-Confidence, New Self-Worth, New Self-Respect and New Self-Love. Those 12 core value discoveries really impacted my life and helped me understand who the old me was so that I could forgive her. I apologized to her for letting her down and allowing my lack of knowledge, faith, and wisdom to contribute to her pain. I came to an understanding that not trusting God and not understanding myself led me down the path of not knowing myself enough to choose the right people in my life. I'm thankful for the healing process which helped to restore me and even though the process took years, my heart was finally healed and restored to the point where I was able to love and marry again.

Because of my journey, I can encourage others to get to know yourself, learn to love yourself, and most importantly, learn how to forgive yourself and others. I consider it such an honor to be able to help at least one person make better decisions, dig deeper into their faith, and trust God. My testimony is proof that salvation, prosperity and happiness is not only available, but it is also attainable, no matter which route is taken to evolve.

Today, I am a beautiful, strong, and amazing woman, deeply rooted in Christ, and enjoying sharing life with my three amazing sons (Tywon, Jabari, and Tyler), and my grandchildren (Alaiya,

Natalie and Nathan). I'm especially grateful and thankful for my village for always having my back along this journey. Special thanks to my parents Michael and Jeanette Nelson, who I thank for my entire life. I owe everything to you.

**Three affirmations that helped me get through, and I hope they help you!**

1. I breathe in courage, I exhale doubt.
2. Peace is not the absence of chaos, but my response to it.
3. Love yourself MORE than your need for love from him! Say it . . . I am enough!

**Three questions I would like to ask to help you in your evolution!**

1. What were the red flags you should have seen and been alerted by?
2. Manipulation is never okay. If someone threatens to kill themselves because you decide to leave them, what should you do? How do you save them WHILE saving yourself and maintain your happiness?
3. When the love is over and the relationship is done, what are you willing to do to reinvent yourself, re-invest in your soul, and create the woman you were truly destined to be?

## **REFLECTIONS FOR YOUR EVOLUTION**

# I Am Stronger Than My Fears!

## Suan-Nesha Fuller Scott

Have you ever been in the middle of something you knew was not meant for you, but you kept trying because you were afraid of failing? Have you ever stayed in a place far too long because you were afraid of being judged? Have you ever tried to hide from the naysayers because you wanted to prove them wrong? I know that feeling all too well. When I met my husband, I was attending graduate school, working full-time every weekend, and taking care of my cousin's children during the weekdays. I had a lot on my plate. I lived with my mother and my sister in a house I helped my mother buy, but that was me! I was the mature and responsible one, who always did the right thing. If I am honest with myself this relationship was my way of escaping.

I was a part of a virtual community that gathered online to socialize, and my husband was a DJ for the chat room. I always asked him why he looked so mean on camera and I encouraged him to smile.

He was a family-oriented man, ten years older than me, and his considerate manner drew me in. I felt I had found my knight in shining armor because of the way he showered me with attention and encouragement. It was my first serious relationship and several people questioned me, "Are you sure this is what you want?" I knew my family thought I had lost my mind when I announced I would be uprooting to move halfway across the country to be with a man I met online. He had a seven-year-old son from a previous marriage, and I did not want him to be separated from his son by so many miles. That was a major factor in my relocation decision. He was committed to and supportive of my move and did not want me to make that kind of transition without a serious commitment, so we became engaged.

Not long after my move, he began to get several anonymous text messages from someone who claimed to be my ex. Initially, I knew nothing about the text messages, but my fiancé kept getting angry with me and I had no clue why. The messages accused me of not being in love with my fiancé and alleged that I belonged to someone else who was going to come to get me and bring me back home. It was just a bunch of lies. Since my aunt was the only person in my family who had his phone number, I told him those messages must be coming from someone he knew, and not from anyone I knew. He told me that he had a discussion with his exes about the text messages and the messages suddenly stopped.

Eventually, his son came to live with us permanently and, together, we all moved to another state. From the time I initially moved to the time we got married, six years had passed and six months before we married, my mother died very unexpectedly.

It was a devastating loss for me and I reached a point in our relationship where I was feeling alone, but I was more afraid of being alone physically. I lost myself in the relationship. I was raised by a single mother who never discussed relationships, sex, or intimacy with me, and I had no clue about how marriage or relationships were supposed to work. I met my biological dad when I was twenty-six, so he was not there during those early years to teach me how a man was supposed to treat me. While I was single, my independent woman mindset served me well, but as a married woman who was used to doing things on her own, that type of mindset did not serve me very well.

My husband shared a lot of stories with me about how well his father treated his mother and his stepmother, and I had an opportunity to experience his father's kindness in the way his father treated me. I even joked with my husband that he was just jealous that his dad loved me more than he loved him. However, the way his father treated his mother and stepmother did not translate into the way my husband treated me. From my perspective, my husband brought a lot of hurt from his first marriage into our relationship, however, this was something he adamantly denied during our marriage counseling sessions. I felt like he was keeping me at arm's length to avoid being hurt and used hurtful words as a defense mechanism, to hurt me before I could hurt him. Even though I also brought my share of insecurities into the relationship, I was still in love with the fantasy of love and believed love alone could get us through anything.

It is very unhealthy to allow feelings to remain bottled up, so with the help of counseling I was able to hone my communication skills in a way that allowed me to be more open and vulnerable in expressing how I felt. When we were in a long-distance relationship, we both agreed that communication was all we had, but once we began living in the same state, the communication faltered.

Our arguments became more frequent, and I was concerned of how they were affecting our kids, so I avoided arguing in front of them. Because I had an understanding about the power of our words, even though he said the most hurtful things to me, I did not verbally retaliate. Things said in anger reflect how one truly feels, but it is not what you say, it's how you say it. After one of my most vulnerable moments of being treated in a hospital for depression and anxiety, rather than encouraging me as I sought help, he approached me as if I were weak, or a failure. That interaction resulted in what he referred to as the slap felt around the world. Before I realized it, I had drawn back my hand and connected it with his cheek. I am not proud of that moment, but the tension was running high.

My husband constantly dismissed my attempts to communicate with him in a manner in which we could both learn and grow. He had adopted a perception and an attitude that he could do nothing right by me. The more I tried to pave a pathway to better communication between us, the more I felt I was not being heard. Eventually, I reverted back to the unhealthy habit of keeping things inside and giving him the silent treatment. I sensed the disconnect in our relationship when his conversations about future plans referenced "I" rather than "we" or "us," and even though I no longer felt safe or protected in our relationship, I settled into a place of complacency. I thought things might get better if I kept trying, but I also felt things would not be so hard if we were truly meant to be. I settled into an uncomfortable space and tolerated what was no longer acceptable to me. Fear caused me to continue overlooking and accepting so many things which were not working for me, and it caused me to stay much longer than I should have.

My husband and I shared a love for music which seemed to be one of the things which connected us. We used song lyrics to express our feelings toward each other and I thought it was cute and sweet when he used to e-mail me expressing his feelings with song lyrics. I did the same, but when my song selections went from sweet and loving to "girl run," I took note of that. In the later years, the songs on my playlist consisted of songs like "Me" by Tamia, "Emotional Rollercoaster" and "Gotta Go Gotta Leave" by Vivian Green, "Listen" by Beyonce, and "Wanna Be Happy" by Kirk Franklin.

When our relationship continued to affect our youngest son's development I knew that I could no longer keep settling for less than we deserved. I sat my husband down and let him know that our relationship was over, but we continued to live under the same roof for another two years. We used the pandemic as the reason why we were still under the same roof, but the truth was, I was afraid of the unknown. At some point I knew continuing to stay would only lead to greater resentment and I no longer wanted to feel stuck in a relationship. If I continued making excuses for not physically separating from my husband, there would never be a change, so my son and I moved in with my younger sister who had just purchased a three-bedroom home.

Less than a month after our separation, my husband had a very serious health scare and for the sake of our sons, I was right there by his side. Once again, I put my needs on the back burner and focused on his, which contributed to my depression and anxiety spiraling out of control. The concern I was showing to him in his time of need was not reciprocated, and I felt my kindness was being taken for weakness. I asked him to stop telling people we were best friends because he did not treat me as a friend. When I found myself in need of the kind of support I showed him, he was certainly not a friend to me. I stood alone.

Forgiveness, they say, is not so much for the benefit of the other person, but rather, forgiveness helps you. I needed to forgive myself, not him, for freely giving him something he was not ready to receive, cherish, or protect. He showed me, by his actions, that he was not capable of giving me what I needed, yet I still stayed. Acts of service is my love language, and my husband said a lot of things that were not backed up by his actions. One of the songs on my playlist contains lyrics which accurately reflected my headspace during that time. The song is "I Wish I Wasn't," by Heather Headley (if you have never heard it, go listen to it). Most of the lyrics were point on and accurate, but I do not wish "I could go back to the day before we met" to "skip my regret."

Who am I as a result of my experiences? I am still a work in progress, battling obstacles every day that try to derail me. Some nights I go to bed feeling beaten down by life as I deal with neurological and physical health issues, job-related stress, and adjusting to life as a single mother to an amazing little boy with different abilities. I am fighting for myself and my son when I set a goal to wake up each morning with a fresh determination and a renewed spirit. I am working to take back my health, my mind, and my life. That relationship taught me a lot about myself. I became more aware of my strengths (what I brought to the table) and my weaknesses (the things I needed to work on), but the most important lesson I learned was to never lose sight of my worth. For more than half of my life I was not truly living, but now my focus has returned to enjoying and living life, being grateful, and raising my son to be the best person he can be.

Have you heard the saying "fear has two meanings: face everything and rise, or fear everything and run?" Which of those meanings will you choose for yourself and your circumstances? It is my prayer that you find the strength and courage to face everything that comes. There will be times when you may fall short, but every morning presents you with an opportunity to go at it again.

I am stronger than my fears, and so are you!! Always remember that!

**Three affirmations that helped me get through, and I hope they help you!**

1. I am stronger than my fears!

2. My self-love and value come from within me, not from the expectations others may have of me. I define my worth!

3. I will not allow myself to become uncomfortable so that others in my life can be comfortable.

**Three questions I would like to ask to help you in your evolution!**

1. The songs on my headspace playlist prompted me to realize it was time to leave that relationship. If you were to create a list of songs or song lyrics that speak to your current headspace, what would be on your song list?

2. What do you envision when you look to your future life? Journal your vision or create a playlist to encourage yourself.

3. Do you know your love language? If not, I challenge you to identify what it is. Journal what you need to feel loved in a relationship and be prepared to express those needs to your partner in a productive way.

*I Am Stronger Than My Fears!*

**REFLECTIONS FOR YOUR EVOLUTION**

# From Pain to Progress

## J. Tyneka Nelson

I was five months pregnant with my second child, and having previously endured infertility issues, the miracle of being pregnant was a blessing. I was scheduled to have an ultrasound the following morning and while I was thinking about it, I whispered a prayer: "Lord, please let this one be a healthy baby boy." My thoughts were interrupted by the vibration of an incoming text message from one of my coworkers which read, "Really? Your husband just came into my banking center and opened his accounts with someone else?"

What was she talking about? I was confused by the text message and just brushed it off. I continued working and told myself I would just respond to her later. Later that evening, when I mentioned the strange text message to my husband, he explained that he did go into the bank to inquire about 529 plans and investment options to secure our children's future. We had those discussions on multiple occasions, so it made perfect sense. I finally responded back to my coworker:

"Girl, you know he would only open up accounts with you. He was only there asking about 529 plans."

She responded back with "What?? Why is he lying? I saw the signature cards! He opened a checking and a savings account."

My attention quickly shifted to my active five-year-old daughter telling me all about her day. I became fully engaged with her and put that last text exchange out of my mind. I entertained my daughter for a while, prepared dinner, and after dinner it was bath time. Story time and then bedtime were a welcome relief because I was exhausted!

That following morning, the ultrasound did not go as we had hoped. Not only did we discover we were we not having a boy, our unborn daughter was diagnosed with Anencephaly, a rare congenital disability. I was overwhelmed by emotions after hearing that report. Along with feelings of guilt, sadness and disappointment, I was also feeling confused and angry. Sharing the diagnosis with only my parents and my sister, we had to make a decision about whether or not to terminate the pregnancy. I had so many questions for God, but for the time being, they had to wait.

The next day one of my best friends, Renee, called me. She didn't sound quite like herself and I wondered if my parents or my sister had shared our news with her. We briefly chatted and then she said to me, "You are a powerful woman, but you never have to suffer in silence. I'm always here for you. I need you and our babies to be stress-free because we have come too far." I was touched by her words and silently wept. She continued the conversation by letting me know that my husband had changed his relationship status on Facebook from married to it's complicated.

I was stunned, confused, and I felt my heart shatter. A knot formed in my throat, I felt sick to my stomach, and I could not speak. I could hear my friend calling my name, but I could not respond. I had no words.

"Hello? Hello? Tyneka, are you still there?" my friend asked.

I knew she was waiting on my response, but I still had no words. My mind went back to the text message I received the day before from my co-worker and I was immediately filled with anger. I told my friend I would call her back and I yelled downstairs to my husband who was sitting at the kitchen table. Standing at the top of the stairs, I asked him about his Facebook status and he jumped out of the chair, knocking it to the floor, slammed his fist on the table, and began cursing and screaming at me!

"I'm not going to do this anymore! I want to be able to come home and relax! I don't want to have to bathe anyone, play with dolls, step over toys, or talk about my day to anyone! I'm leaving!"

I stood there in disbelief. My heart was overcome with fear at the thought of being a single mother and the shame associated with admitting my marriage failed. As he continued to rant and rave, my mind was bombarded with thoughts of what it would be like to live alone, but at the same time, I knew I would not be raising my children in a home with unhealthy communication, bickering, and fighting. I was not going to raise my girls to think a man should treat a woman the way their father was treating me. It was an unacceptable message to send and I would not allow my daughters to believe it was an appropriate narrative for love. I decided right then and there that it was time for me to go. That was not the first time he had raised his voice at me, disrespected, or belittled me, but it was going to be the last time I accepted it.

Before I could complete and process my thoughts, I heard him on the phone with two of his siblings, Mario and Tolester.

"I need you to come right now! I'm moving out right now. Hurry up!"

After he hung up with his brothers, he directed his rage back at me while he frantically packed his clothes.

"I going to be so happy now that I am rid of you!"

He continued to hurl insults at me as he faced his demons, while I just stood there feeling broken. I felt my chest tighten and I could hardly breathe. I thought about my unborn child as I felt a sensation of razor blades cutting through my stomach. All of a sudden, I grabbed my car keys and ran out of the house. My first instinct was to call my sister who agreed to immediately come meet me. There was no way I was going to allow my daughter to come home from school and witness such chaos, so I also made arrangements for my sister to pick her up after school. After I was done talking with my sister, I just drove around for about thirty minutes trying to process what had just happened.

After driving around for a while, I decided to return home to see if my husband, Paxton, had calmed down. My sister was already there when I pulled up, and one of his brothers had also arrived and was helping to pack things into the car. My husband was still angry and causing a huge scene for all our neighbors to witness while I sat in my car with my sister recounting the whirlwind of events which happened in the past two days. When I began to talk about the text messages from my co-worker, my unborn child's diagnosis, learning about the Facebook status which was changed to it's complicated, I could tell by looking at my sister it was not a very good idea for her to be there at that moment.

I continued to watch my husband load up his car, but I did not care about any of the material things he was taking. As far as I was concerned, he could have it all. My girls and I would still have a roof over our heads and I had a job and money in the bank to begin rebuilding. Suddenly it hit me like a head-on collision. I logged onto my online banking and my balance was twenty-three cents! My husband had taken it all!! I had just gotten paid, so he took my last regular paycheck, which included my bonus, and all of the savings. He planned the whole thing, and I was outraged!

That sleepless night turned into saddened days, which turned into tearful and depression-filled weeks and months. There were many days when it was a struggle just to get out of bed, and even though I somehow managed to accomplish my daily tasks as a mother, I was not always mentally and emotionally present. Single parenthood was not my desired path, but it was my new path, so I had to own it.

During our time of separation, my husband experienced many life-altering events. He experienced the loss of a parent, the loss of a job and home, and he had to endure multiple health concerns. I had compassion for him as the father of my children and reached out to offer help. Whether I was offering food, money, sheltering options or job opening opportunities, my efforts of goodwill were never well-received. As often as I extended an olive branch of peace, my husband returned the branch to me it with the olives fallen off and the branches trampled under his feet.

One night, as I lay in bed, I petitioned God to take the hatred, anger, bitterness, sadness, hurt, and pain away. I used to walk with such confidence, grace, and strength. What happened to me? Where had I disappeared to? Who was the person impersonating me? The next morning, my mother, who is a woman of faith, called to check on me. She shared with me the importance of forgiving my husband for the sake of my own peace. My parents had always instilled strength, endurance, wisdom, and Christian values in me; however, the person I had become was not a good representation of the mother, woman, daughter, sister, or friend I knew I was. A desire to be a good example for my daughter motivated me to do something I did not feel like doing. The way I handled difficult situations was the blueprint I was laying out for my daughter to follow, so I pressed through the hardship in my life so my daughter would have a positive example of what it means to endure with Christian values, grace, and elegance.

Placing one foot on the floor, I told myself I would take all of the negative feelings and energy and use it for good. As I put my other foot on the floor, I promised myself I would push harder than I ever had in my life. I was going to love harder than I had ever loved, laugh harder than I had ever laughed, and live more than I had ever lived. My success would be my most significant benefit and revenge, so I positioned myself for success by writing out affirmations and strategically placing them throughout my house. I wanted to be surrounded by positive reinforcement on every turn as I embarked on the next phase of my healing and success journey. That next phase was forgiveness.

The act of forgiveness is often misunderstood. Forgiveness means releasing someone of wrongdoing in exchange for your own freedom. To evolve into the woman I wanted to be, forgiveness was in order, so with a glass of wine in one hand and my pen in the other, I wrote down a list of names and the corresponding act of wrongdoing. I listed those who gave unsolicited advice and opinions, those who lied, and those who assassinated my character in an attempt to discredit my parenting skills, during the divorce and child custody proceedings. My list grew as I added anyone who attempted to tear me down as a professional or in any way tried to harm me. It was time to let go of everything I had already held onto for too long. I asked God to have mercy on their souls and strengthen them as they became my footstools, and with that single act, I resolved that toxicity would no longer have a place in my life.

On another sheet of paper, I wrote out my "single mother vision" along with my personal, educational, spiritual, emotional, financial, and professional goals. On my timeline, the first and most important goal was loving me and unapologetically walking in my truth daily. That one goal not only saved my life, but it gave me a new and improved life. Being patient and extending grace to myself gave me the ability to organically love the person staring back at me in the mirror, imperfect with flaws and all.

My evolution took years to manifest, but I was worth every moment I poured into it. The future of my daughter was depending upon my evolution, so I led the way. I re-enrolled in college and graduated with a Bachelor of Science in Business Administration and a Master of Science in Business Administration with a concentration in Information Technology. My dream of becoming an entrepreneur became a reality and I began to build my family's legacy. To honor my daughter, I formed The Jazmeen Miles Anencephaly Foundation Inc., a non-profit organization dedicated to assisting families dealing with congenital infant disabilities. My event planning business is flourishing (A Moment In Time Event Planning LLC), and I enjoy creating the perfect travel experience for my clients as the founder and CEO of JJ & T Travel Management Group LLC. As I evolved, I continued to expand my skillset, increased my community involvement through service, and continued to advance in my professional career while working for a Fortune 500 company.

It took ten years to heal and rebuild, and when I was finally ready to share my life with someone special, I quickly adapted to modern society's dating scene. I was mindful not to introduce anyone I was dating to my family, especially my daughter, unless I was confident he was the one for me. When I finally introduced the extraordinary man, Dre, who I eventually married to my family, my ex-husband petitioned the court in an attempt to keep him away from my daughter.

The court denied that petition, but the lessons I learned through the process of my evolution helped me to move past those types of attempts to disturb my peace or distract me from loving and being loved. My focus remained on my complete happiness, and I loved myself no matter what the challenges to my peace were.

When I remarried, my ex-husband continued attempts to cause division within my newly-blended family. He tried to infuse my daughter's mind with negativity by telling her things like "No other man can love you like I can," and "Your mother is trying to replace your daddy; that other man is not your daddy." Those types of statements introduce harm, confusion, and insecurity into the heart of a child, and no child should ever feel a need to choose who to love or be told or overhear negative statements about their parents.

My motherly philosophy is, "If Mommy is not well, the kids are not well; therefore, Mommy must be well, and well she shall be." I had to take a stand. I decided to love myself enough to not allow my ex-husband, his family, or anyone else to hinder me from living my life to its fullest. I chose to love myself beyond my flaws and continue to excel, despite what anyone else believed about me. In my early evolution phase, I preserved my sanity by constantly remind myself that another person's thoughts, views, or opinions about me or my life was in no way reflective of my reality. It was not necessary for me to defend my decisions or cower behind the perspectives of other people. I stayed focused on my goals and repudiated negative energy, opinions, and thoughts, which were nothing more than distractions.

My new husband and I welcomed our newest daughter into the family and four years later, I finally got my boy! He is a four-legged Doberman who we call Rocky. We purchased a home in the country and plan to live there and enjoy life with each other. We are both passionate about our family and future together and hold that close to our hearts. As we allow God to teach us what it means to submit to each other, our love has the ability to persevere beyond temporary feelings and is yielding beautiful results.

I am still a work in progress, but I am evolving daily. I have come a long way from being the broken woman I was many years ago. I survived the pain and trauma associated with a broken marital relationship and unpleasant custody battle which lasted for years. I have overcome depression, embarrassment, loss, and financial hardship, but when God replenishes and restores things in your life, only He knows what you need. If you are going through a trying time in your life right now, please know that others have experienced the same thing, if not worse, and came out on the winning side. Write your goals and vision for your life, state your affirmations and intentions each day, put in the hard work even when you don't feel like it, and watch your life begin to change. Fix your crown, Queen, because you got this! I'm here to let you in on a secret: Sis, the love is over, not you!

**Three affirmations that helped me get through, and I hope they help you!**

1. Today I am a better version of myself than I was yesterday

2. I love myself and I unapologetically walk in my truth today and every day

3. In Christ, I am okay; therefore, everyone and everything attached to me is okay.

**Three questions that I would like to ask you to help you in your evolution!**

1. Are you currently the person you desire to be?

2. What does forgiveness look like to you, and have you forgiven whoever you need to forgive?

3. What are your goals and vision for your life?

## REFLECTIONS FOR YOUR EVOLUTION

# Self-inflicted Drowning

## Venus J. Jackson

*"My heart will always remember when I was drowning, the ones who held their hand out to pull me from the deep and the ones who pretended not to see a thing."*
-Author Stephanie Bennett-Henry

### Pillar I: Why

Synchronized swimming is a lot like a marriage. It is a craft that contains several components such as graceful and coordinated movements, strength and discipline, along with endurance, effort and desire. If any one of those components is off-balance, a marriage will begin to flounder, much like in synchronized swimming. After ingesting the proverbial chlorine-filled water into your lungs, your eyes will begin the slow burn of seeing your drowning marriage. Weighed down by the fatigue from the constant fighting, water will pull you under and take your hopes and your marriage along with it. I have compared my marriage to synchronized swimming because although it was harmonious at times, what was required to pull it off was an unimaginable amount of work for both partners. Synchronized swimming and self-inflicted emotional drowning are in so many ways similar to a relationship that nearly killed my inner spirit!

I know I closed my eyes to the red neon flags which were flapping uncontrollably on any given day. I had somehow convinced myself that wanting to rear my children in a two-parent home and provide them with a stable environment, reminiscent of what I had experienced growing up, was what made me keep blinders on for nearly two decades. I used that one solitary desire as fuel to help me push past the first few years of what were a million small neon flags. I had equated our early conflicts to us simply being young and polar opposites. Scientifically, opposites are supposed to attract, but in our case, it was a hard no! During our time of over sixteen years together, we learned both heartbreaking and heart-healing lessons.

Our parents were hopeful we would work past the bigger challenges in our relationship, and so were we, but having such opposite views on marriage, finances, or even dreams, presented a significant issue. Compromise is an essential component of marriage but divorcing your unwavering and deep-seated beliefs inside of a marriage is something completely different. Doing so merely becomes the start of the self-inflicted drowning process and unfortunately, most of us do not realize this until we are already waist-deep in the water.

### Hotel or Cell Phone?

There may be times when you feel you are putting in one thousand percent effort, but to your spouse, it may feel like you have only given one percent. From my perspective, I was the one giving my one thousand percent and my husband was giving one percent. It was his sneaky behavior which played a role in my inability to trust him, along with his verbally abusive behavior which was present in our relationship for a while.

My husband had a knack for hiding things for no apparent reason. He hid information, finances, and even snacks. Yes, snacks. Who knew that his pattern of behavior was the foreshadowing of something more sinister? I had no concrete evidence of his infidelity, other than a strong hunch, his duplicitous behavior, an unexplained hotel receipt.

I asked my husband to explain the hotel receipt which was from a town I had certainly never been to which displayed a date and time when I would have been working. In addition, the date and time displayed was during a time when my husband should have been sleeping. He worked twelve hours on the graveyard shift, so his routine was repetitious. Work, shower, wind down, sleep, eat, and do it all again the next day. As far as I was concerned, my little investigation was complete when the hotel charges appeared on our bank statement.

As I continued to question him about the receipt and the charge which appeared on our bank statement, the conversation escalated into an argument. I reached for his cell phone to make a point, and BAM!! A closed fist to my face inflicted horror, shock, and disdain that has remained in my memory for well over a decade.

What in the hell had just happened? My husband had never put his hands on me like that, so why at that moment? What was in that cell phone that he did not want to be discovered? What was so private that he was willing to punch me in my face to protect? What or who was worth him losing his wife over?

I had always believed in holding people accountable for their actions, and my husband was no exception. My life partner had violated me in a way I could not have ever seen coming, let alone forgive; I was hurt to my very core. Yes, I called 911 and yes, I pressed charges. I put him out and made him handle his transgressions through the legal system. I sought counseling immediately because I knew I would never look at him or any other man the same if I did not take that step towards counseling. I watched him walk through the fire he had brought upon himself. He attended anger management counseling sessions and continued to honor his commitment and obligations to our family. I can attest that putting in the work can restore even a broken marriage. After a ten-month separation, my husband and I reconciled and both agreed to put forth the effort necessary to make our marriage work. We both experienced the damage caused by the cell phone incident and witnessed how deeply it cut into our already fragile relationship. The memory of that experience left an enormous crack in our already rocky foundation. The months and years that followed were not easy, but we were both committed to the process.

## Pillar II: When

*"You made that choice to improve yourself for a reason. Don't go backwards to habits and situations that weren't helping you evolve. You have to keep reminding yourself why you even decided to move forward. Stay positive about what's to come by being consistent with your change."* -Author @idillionaire/Twitter

### The Twelve English Letters . . . Mom Knew Best!

Our parents were always offering advice, having the conversations with us, and praying for us, but I will bypass letting them know they were usually always right. I was treading in the murky waters of fear for quite a while. I was afraid of the unknown and I was stuck in a place, marking time, constantly thinking about how I was going to make it on my own. When I finally admitted to myself that I was fearful, and the reason why I was fearful, I was ready to reach out to my parents and admit I was experiencing the unhappiness they had already seen coming.

For many years after the cell phone incident, things seemed to be headed in the right direction. We attended both traditional and religious-based counseling, but between his uncommunicative habits, my high expectations, and the cell phone nightmare, I made a very difficult decision. It was not an overnight decision, but it seemed to me that it was more harmful to everyone involved to remain married with things being the way they were. I evaluated my life, had countless conversations with my parents and grandparents, and I used all the tools which had been provided to me over the years. I wanted my children to know what a great marriage looked like, but their father and I were not providing them with the best possible view of what that should look like. Facing the shame of my failure as a wife, his failure as a husband, and our failure as a married couple, my decision to end our marriage boiled down to my desire to receive inner peace.

We agreed upon a specific separation date, and I began preparing myself for the day when my husband would be leaving. I established a strict budget, began working two jobs, saved money, and made specific arrangements in anticipation of that date. Unfortunately, the closer we got to the separation date, the more life was continuing to happen. We experienced multiple family deaths, a car accident, and everything else imaginable which hindered our progress. What was once a fixed move out date became an involuntarily flexible date.

When my mother was lying in the hospital bed with tubes down her throat during the last three weeks of her life, my heart, mind, and soul came into full alignment. The worst thing ever was happening to me, my mother was dying, and my husband did not come to the hospital until her final hours. During the last three weeks of her life, my friends, family, and even a co-worker found time in those three weeks to come, but not him. The feeling of abandonment that settled inside of me was as fierce as a raging fire. Regardless of what our marital status was, my blood boiled at the thought of not being supported by my spouse during such a critical time. He left me alone to deal with the thought of losing my mother, while I was also lending emotional support to my father and my children.

As my mother laid on her hospital bed, unable to speak, but still able to write, she wrote a final decree for me in a simple message. She simply wrote: "*Go and be happy.*" It's ironic how four little words, twelve English letters, and the loss of my mother, changed my entire perspective, level of enthusiasm, and emotional well-being for the better. That simple declaration, from my mother, was all the motivation I needed.

It was time to act on what had always been directly in front of me. I dug deep and re-evaluated, once again, how I would keep myself from drowning. My budget continued to be my focus as I saved as much as I could. Cutting out the extras, enabled me to see how I could actually run my household as a single parent on just my income. While I was working on my budget, I was also working on getting to know myself. I considered what I wanted for myself and the steps necessary to make my present evolve into my envisioned future. My planning and preparation went far beyond just changing the door locks. I had to prepare my children mentally and emotionally and I had to clear out my emotional closet. The memories of our better days as a couple were placed in their proper place, a memory box. I could not operate from a place of clarity until my level of stress was under control, and as I continued to move forward, the most important element of my security was to get my spiritual life in order. Any marriage which God did not put together was never destined to stand. Ultimately, I had to realize that the end my marriage was not the end of my spirit; I simply needed to reset with God. A valuable lesson learned throughout my experience was that removal does not mean defeat. When I became courageous enough to press past the fear of the unknown, I realized I was strong enough to step out on faith.

## *Pillar III: Forgiveness*

"It took me a long time to understand what it means to forgive someone. I always wondered how I could forgive someone who chose to hurt me. But after a lot of soul searching, I realized that forgiveness is not about accepting or excusing their behavior. It is about letting it go and preventing their behavior from destroying my heart." -Author unknown

## *Comparison Can Be the Thief of Joy*

Pain is inevitable; suffering is optional. This is most definitely something I wish I had learned within the first few years of marriage because I would have definitely bypassed the optional suffering! My parents and grandparents have been together for over forty years and I have observed them managing whatever life threw at their individual marriages. The way they modeled marriage and commitment in front of me became my gold standard. While writing this chapter, I realized that my marriage experience was based on the after-effect of their work; their synchronized portions, if you will. I never knew the depth of the content of any of their conversations, arguments, or the compromises they made for the sake of their marriages. I only saw the beauty in what had been created and presented. Much like synchronized swimming, the showing was what I had fantasized about emulating most. Yes, I say fantasized because, I can admit, that is simply what it was. I compared what I deemed to be a mess of a marriage to a gold standard and it was never going to live up to what I thought it should have been. Forgiveness was in order, but in my discovery, I realized I had to first forgive myself for setting my marriage goals as high as I had, and then forgive myself for remaining underwater for as long as I did. I extended forgiveness to myself for not seeking the inner healing I needed because until I was healed, I did not have the capacity to even consider forgiving him. Taking those important measures allowed me to reach the surface and clear the chlorine from my eyes. Next up was getting it out of my lungs!

## *Pillar IV: Healing*

"Trauma creates change you do not choose. Healing is about creating change you do choose." -Michelle Rosenthal

## *The Evolution Changed Us All*

I like to credit my evolution to the healing of my total life experiences. I did the work to put the lingering traumas of my life in their proper place, which is the past. My failed marriage taught me how to handle the bad moments, but it also taught me how to appreciate the good moments. It taught me tolerance, patience, and the benefit of emotional honesty. My ability to give unyielding forgiveness and receive peace did not come until later in my journey, but an unlikely friendship opened the door to my freedom. When I cultivated a friendship with who I now refer to as my best friend, that friendship proved to be very instrumental in my healing. I was thankful for the guidance and support of a friend who held me accountable for working through the hurt and allowing me to freely express my pain through the process.

It was this special friendship which not only helped me to see where I went wrong but exposed me to the possibilities of experiencing something real, something tangible, something raw, and something unconditional. Through that friendship, I was rescued from the ocean of emotional self-inflicted drowning and was able to see how I had been going through the motions of living and loving. I realized I had not been breathing and was surviving on the fumes provided by the love of my children and the desire to be the best parent I could. Through the friendship of one who unselfishly shared his own drowning experience and his healing journey, along with my willingness to do the self-work, I learned that although the love in my marriage had not been enough to sustain it, I was enough!

## Turning Fear into Faith

I had been so fearful and concerned about depriving my children of a two-parent upbringing, but my children are thriving, happy and well-adjusted. The entire family needs to endure the process of healing through a divorce, and each of us learned about peace and self-love on our journey from heartbreak to heart healing.

## Self-inflicted Drowning

My heart smiles knowing that my children have healthy relationships with both of their parents and support the lives we each have gone on to live. I am grateful that my fear turned into faith, and I am grateful that I am still evolving. I walk in forgiveness and peace, which is a continuous journey and not a destination.

Although my husband and I are no longer a couple, we have done the work to remain a family and function as a much better unit co-parenting than we ever did while married. We occasionally do things together with the children, and I can honestly say that therapy and honest conversation can be the healer of surface and deep wounds.

I am proud of the person I have become as a direct result of having married, failed, and looked hard at my role in our unsynchronized marriage. I have learned to talk things out and even listen, which is something we struggled with during our marriage.

I still believe in the idea of love and marriage and have learned to watch out for the pitfalls. I know what I want in a spouse and understand that simply marrying someone for the potential they possess or setting gold standards by which to measure marriage is unrealistic. I've learned the hard lesson that ignoring neon flags will undoubtedly lead to a disruption of harmony, and I've also learned that love does not always come packaged in a pretty box with an elaborately decorative bow on top. Love sometimes is just plain ugly, and you must work to find its beauty. Love takes two people on the same page with common goals, digging deep, and having the fortitude to remain in sync while recognizing when the other one needs to come up for air.

It is okay to be out of sync with your partner and it is okay to press reset on your marriage after dealing with a traumatic event. It is also most important to be able to recognize the moment when you begin to drown in the marriage. Seek help before the water reaches your waist and don't be afraid to walk, run or swim on your own. Understand that a failed marriage does not define you, it merely refines you. You will learn soon enough that even on your own, you are enough!

**Three affirmations that helped me get through, and I hope they help you!**

1. Today, I choose healing!
2. I am evolving every day and in every way.
3. I AM ENOUGH!

**Three questions I would like to ask you to help you in your evolution!**

1. Being hyper-focused on one area of my life while neglecting some other aspects caused me to ignore several neon flags. What red or neon flags have you overlooked?
2. At what point in your relationship did you notice you were drowning?
3. When you noticed you were drowning, what was your initial reaction and what steps did you take to save yourself?

*Evolve*

**REFLECTIONS FOR YOUR EVOLUTION**

# The Voice from the Backseat

## Kerrie L. Brittingham

"Mommy, why are you always so sad and mad at me?" An innocent little voice from the back seat halted all my thoughts, made my heart sink, brought tears to my eyes, and brought clarity to a decision I had been contemplating. All I could think about was, "How is it possible that my eight-year-old son is carrying the load of my toxic marriage and placing the blame on himself?" At that moment, I knew I needed to find the courage to do what I had to do. What did that mean for our futures? What did that mean for our home? What did that mean for my children's well-being?

Up until that point, I had chosen to ignore all the other signs which were pointing towards change that needed to happen. However, I could not ignore that little, yet extremely loud voice coming from the backseat of my vehicle. That voice is now fourteen years old, but to this day, I still hear that little eight-year-old voice reminding me to stay the course.

On the day I finally made the decision to move forward with the divorce process, I woke up at 4:30 a.m. as usual. Before leaving for bootcamp, I woke my husband and asked him the same thing I had asked him on numerous occasions.

"Will you attend marriage counseling sessions with me?"

His response was the same as always, "No! It's not my problem, it's your problem. If you need help, go get help and I don't want to hear about it again!"

That conversation played over and over in my head as I drove to bootcamp and questions flooded my mind.

Why won't he go to marriage counseling?

Why am I and this marriage not important enough to him?

Why won't he at least do it for the sake of our children?

What have I done wrong?

Why am I not good enough?

Why? Why? Why?

While I was running that morning mile, I used the time to pray and pump myself up to pull the trigger. Pulling the trigger was hearing myself say, "I want a divorce." That morning, I ran my fastest mile and had one of my best workouts! I didn't want the bootcamp to end because I knew I had to go back home and face reality. The reality was, my husband and I had been together for twenty-three years and had been married for the past nine of those years. On the drive back home, so many memories, good and bad, from the past twenty-three years filled my thoughts and the closer I got to home, the louder the little voice of my son played over and over in my head. I was nauseous and a bit overtaken by anxiety, but I found the courage, once I got in the house, to tell my husband I decided to file for divorce. He kind of chuckled and brushed me off.

I was annoyed by his response, as if he didn't take me seriously, but he had become so accustomed to me setting boundaries over the years and not reinforcing them, why would he think things would be any different that time? I was determined to follow through with the divorce. For the sake of my emotional and mental health as well as that of my children, I had to somehow bring about a change. My children were being raised in a toxic home environment, getting first-hand exposure to what an unhealthy relationship looked like. I did not want that to become normal for them, so my mind was already made up. I told him I was serious and I went on about my day.

I was in a fog all that day, and by the end of the day my husband was saying everything I had already heard him say before. He said he would go to counseling, yet hours earlier, he told me he wouldn't go. He told me he would begin attending church with me and the kids, which is a promise he made long before the kids were even born, yet he never honored his word. He promised to be and do everything I had been asking for years, but I had no more confidence in him. In times past, I would have taken him at his word, buried my head in the sand and moved on, but I was on a mission and did not allow his false promises to derail my focus. The courage I needed to stand firm and not bury my head was constantly replaying in my mind in the form of that little voice from the back seat.

The decision to file for divorce was an emotional ride filled with questions. I reflected on the healthy model of love my parents presented before me and my brother, but I had almost become oblivious to what love truly was. I didn't know what to expect when I embarked on my divorce journey, but I knew it had to be better than the journey I was on.

I was a therapist to so many who came to me to help them navigate their journeys, yet, there I was being tossed around by my emotions, seemingly unable to navigate my own journey before me. I found security in one thing; my kids and I were not alone. I had my parents, my brother, a few close friends, and my relationship with God to be my strength when I didn't feel like I had enough strength to go on.

The next day, I placed one of the hardest calls I have ever had to make. I called my parents to let them know of my decision to file for divorce, and the moment I heard my momma's voice on the other end of the phone I broke down crying. I felt like such a failure and was afraid my parents would be disappointed in me, but that was far from the truth. They comforted me, reassured me, and offered their support. I was so relieved, but my next question was "How do we tell the kids?" Yes, I was the therapist who helped countless other children and families navigate life's challenges, but it was different because it just so happened to be my stuff I was trying to navigate through.

We agreed to tell our kids that although mommy and daddy could no longer live together, we would still always be family and they would always be loved. We assured them they would see us both every day and they would not be uprooted from their home. In an attempt to ease the transition, we told them daddy would get them off the bus each day and stay with them at the house until mommy got home from work. They listened with blank stares on their faces and neither of them had much to say. I was heartbroken!

During the transition, I was bombarded with feelings of emotional, mental, financial, and physical self-doubt. I was full of anxiety on every level as I worried about how I would be able to continue to work full-time, pursue my dream of opening my private practice, and still be a good mom! I was overwhelmed with thoughts about how I could continue to provide therapy and guidance to others when my marriage had failed. I was absolutely terrified!

I experienced lighter moments and emotions which seemed to lift me up and bring a sense of relief and empowerment. My children would no longer have to experience the toxic relationship between their dad and me and I would no longer have to fulfill the sexual expectations of someone who did not make me feel as if I existed outside of the bedroom. Those feelings of empowerment helped me through so many dark days and nights. I was motivated to do what I had to do, not only for the sake of my children, but for the sake of everyone involved. Each time I came home from work and wanted to share my day and my husband told me he was not interested in my job and "go find someone else to talk to," I was pushed further away. For almost a year before I made the decision to move forward with the divorce, I no longer wanted to go home if my husband was there. I began going out more with friends and, as a way to cope with the disappointment and emotional turmoil, I began drinking too much. I found opportunities to work late and did anything I could to feel competent, heard, or valued. At home, I felt none of those things. In that one year alone, I lost myself more than I had in all the years of our marriage. We had become strangers living under the same roof.

Before I made my final decision to proceed with divorce, I reflected on my rock bottom moment. One night while attending a birthday celebration, I drank way too much and exhibited some type of behavior which caused me to lose one of my dearest friends. To this day, I still don't know what transpired, but it was enough for me to realize I had reached a point where I knew I needed to "deal with my shit." I was time for me to stop hiding behind drinking, work, and whatever else was hindering me from focusing on being a better version of myself.

I shut out the world and focused on my inner healing, being a better mom, and launching my private practice. That phase of my journey was extremely difficult and I often became stuck in the role of victim. I replayed in my mind everything that was done to me, not only in the marriage, but before marriage. I replayed the infidelity, the harsh words spoken, the drug dealing, and the emotional disconnect. The victim mentality tried to hold me hostage as I reflected on the years of dealing with the narcissistic behavior, and the emotional and mental abuse which accompanies such behavior. I needed help to transition from victim to survivor and I found the help I needed when made a ten-hour drive to Myrtle Beach to attend a weekend healing retreat. The long drive gave me ample time to think about what might be ahead for me as I entertained anxious thoughts about what the retreat experience would be like. The retreat was being led by one of my graduate school colleagues, but I was stepping completely outside of my comfort zone by staying at a beach house with six other women who I did not know. When it was time to return home from the retreat, I knew I had begun a new chapter in my life. I left that retreat with six new sisters, six new additions to my village of support, and I was so thankful!

After that weekend, I no longer looked at what was done to me or what I lost, but rather, I saw the lessons learned, the growth I had experienced, and everything I gained through the most difficult time in my life. As I continue to progress through my journey, I am learning about the many layers of forgiveness while learning more about myself.

Forgiving myself was like ripping off a band-aid. It hurt! I forgave myself for resorting to drinking as a coping mechanism which not only took time away from my children, but it caused me to ruin a precious friendship. I had to take full responsibility for the consequences of the pain I caused and respect the boundaries established for our relationship, but I'm thankful to still be able to witness her dreams coming true (albeit through social media). Forgiveness is a healing process, and as I continue to forgive myself for being the one who filed for divorce, I am finding peace in a home which is no longer toxic. Staying in the marriage for so long and becoming consumed with anger and resentment was another area where I had to extend forgiveness to myself. By allowing anger and resentment to build, I could not be the wife I wanted to be. Guiding my children through their forgiveness journey has been exceptionally challenging.

My daughter was extremely hurt when her father moved away to Florida, and she expresses her pain in anger. He has been physically present in her life since that time on very few occasions and I am emotionally torn as I watch her cope with the pain of her disappointment. There are times when I experience the same anger because I believe my children deserve better, so I understand when she chooses to shut her father out altogether. As much as my heart aches for her, I constantly remind myself that I can help my children navigate their feelings, but I am in no way responsible for their feelings.

As I continue to connect with myself, I have been able to make our house a home again. I am more mentally and emotionally present and my confidence has been restored. My private practice is flourishing, and even though I am divorced, I am still trusted by my clients to lead them to victory on their journey. Being able to love myself positioned me to being able to receive love!

After the divorce, I told my mother I was going to remain single for the rest of my life. At the time, I didn't feel I could ever receive love again, but she did not want me to shut love out at such a young age. The more I allowed myself to heal, the more my heart opened to even the thought of loving again. When I was invited out to lunch by a gentleman who was in town on a work assignment, I thought "What the heck, a free lunch sounds good." Little did I know that lunch date would result in me learning what it was like to be truly loved by someone else. It was during that year-long season of long-distance dating when I learned to trust again. Because of my experience with infidelity within a relationship, I was challenged in the area of trusting again, but I persevered. Our relationship continued to grow as he exercised all the patience necessary to allow me the space and the pace to allow someone else to be a part of my life. When he relocated to Kentucky, it opened the door for my children to experience a healthy relationship. He was not my happiness, but he added tremendously to my happiness. In my previous marriage, that was one of the mistakes I made. I expected him to be my happiness and I lost sight of what my happiness looked like.

There is no timeline for healing and forgiveness, there is no instruction booklet, and there is no easy path. Allow yourself to feel what you are feeling and ask yourself how you can shift to change how you are feeling. Tap into your senses. When I tapped into my sense of hearing, I will be forever thankful for the little, yet very loud voice from the backseat!

**Three affirmations that helped me get through, and I hope they help you!**

1. I am allowed to move past the things and people who no longer bring positivity to my life.
2. I believe things will always work out, even when it doesn't feel like it.
3. Everything is unfolding in perfect timing, I trust, I believe, I receive.

**Three questions I would like to ask you to help you in your evolution!**

1. What am I teaching those around me by my behaviors and actions?
2. What am I doing to become a survivor and no longer a victim?
3. What have I learned about myself?

*The Voice from the Backseat*

# *REFLECTIONS FOR YOUR EVOLUTION*

# I Believed He Was Everything I Wanted

## Dwan Warren

Breaking the cycle of dysfunction and toxic relationships was easier said than done. There were lessons I needed to learn because I was tired of hurting, feeling alone, and feeling as though I was not valued. Throughout my first marriage, which was riddled with deception, infidelity, and abuse, I acquired a bittersweet reminder of how important it is to know your identity, know what love is, and the power of setting healthy boundaries.

I fondly remember my childhood daydreams of becoming a wife and a mother. I imagined the beautiful wedding day, raising and taking care of my children, and keeping a neat and tidy home. In my mind, I saw myself inviting family and friends over for dinner and creating great memories. Even though that dream did not manifest in my first marriage, I was willing to give love a second chance. I was not going to let the failure of my marriage keep me from being the kind and considerate person I had always been. I believed if you treated people right, loved them passionately, and served without expecting anything in return, it would be reciprocated. That's what I believed, so I was not afraid to try again, and with my heart wide open, I still remember the first time I ever laid eyes on him.

I was out with my girlfriends and sitting right across from me was a very tall and handsome guy with a huge personality which I found attractive. I leaned over to ask my girlfriend who he was and without hesitation he introduced himself to me. I was captivated by his infectious smile, and the tone of his voice was genuinely welcoming. Two weeks passed before our paths crossed again and during that encounter, he asked for my phone number. I played it cool, but I could not wait to tell my girlfriend he has asked for my number. I anxiously awaited his call!

Even before our first date, I noticed several familiar patterns which were the same red flags I ignored and made excuses for during my first marriage. We were just beginning to get to know one another, so I gave him the benefit of the doubt, even though I was doubting. We dated for a little over three years before we got married, and I simply believed everything would work out if I remained steadfast in my love for him. I thought a steadfast love was what he needed to cause him to change his ways and I also believed his heart towards me would change once we got married. The day before our wedding, one of my best friends called pleading with me to not marry him.

She was concerned that he was not the right fit for me. My best friend was aware from the beginning of our relationship, when we first met, and she had observed how it had evolved. From her perspective, she witnessed the same red flags and tried to intervene in what she saw as future heartbreak.

The red flags waved when he made statements like "There's nothing wrong with lying, everyone lies."

The flags continued to wave privately and publicly, when he made fun of my looks, my body, my faith and what I believed, and even joked about how nice I was! He used my kindness as an opportunity to take advantage of me and then he criticized me for not being more assertive.

I challenged myself to understand what love truly was because I was constantly trying to prove to him that I was worthy of being loved by him. When our conversations led to the topic of marriage, he saw marriage as just a piece of paper, but I regarded marriage as a lifelong union honoring God and each other.

He was also very guarded when it came to his social media interactions. His claim was he wanted to protect his privacy, but I couldn't help but notice he never identified his relationship status. As much as I agreed with him wanting to protect his privacy, it bothered me that he was hiding his relationship with me from the other women he was communicating with.

One of those women befriended me through my social media page and we became "mutual friends". We had frequent conversations, one day I mentioned who I was dating. From that point, our conversations became less frequent. When I mentioned the conversation, I was having with our "mutual friend," he became agitated that we were even communicating. My intuition kicked in, and although I knew something was going on, I did not want to embrace the alarm sounding off in my heart. A year later, I was devastated by the news that she was pregnant with his child, which is when she blocked me from her social media page.

When I found out, he pleaded with me to not walk away. He apologized to me and my daughter with flowers and a card. I felt so stupid being in that situation because I did not want to be with a man who I knew was unfaithful. I wanted to stay and prove to her that he loved me after all. I was angry at myself for wanting to stay instead of walking away. I knew then that I needed to wake up, but I did not want to let him go.

When my girlfriend called me pleading with me to call off the wedding, she did it out of her heartfelt love for me. I completely understood her point of view, but in my mind, I had already invested too much time and energy into the relationship to walk away from it one day before the wedding. I held fast to the belief that he would change, and in my heart, I was willing to take the risk. I was determined to keep "loving" and believing that in the end, everything would be alright.

The early months of our marriage were rough. I worked several jobs and still needed financial help from my family and friends. My husband was frustrated about the way things were going, but he found solace in connecting with his social media friends, including the one who had carried his first child. The communication skills between my husband and I were not the best and, in an effort to help improve our relationship, I wanted to pursue marital counseling. My husband was never open to that.

One Friday evening as I was leaving work, I waddled toward the door and down the stairs. I was five months pregnant at the time and I knew it was scorching hot outside because the moment I stepped into the lobby, I could no longer feel the cool air from the office. I kept looking through the glass doors for my husband who had not yet arrived to pick me up from work. I began to panic and didn't quite know whether I should be angry or worried that maybe something bad had happened. I could not reach him on the phone and could not think of any reason for him to be late picking me up. My pregnancy was a high-risk pregnancy, so I tried to remain as calm as possible. When my husband finally arrived to pick me up I was so upset, and he could tell. As I approached the car, I saw him shuffling to change the radio station, looking as if he had just gotten out of bed. The moment I sat in the car I smelled sex all over him and all over the car. He offered no explanation or apology for being late and expressed no empathy or remorse. I knew he had been with *her* and I was enraged and humiliated.

When we got home, I did not say a word; I just allowed that anger, frustration, and hurt to fester. Eventually, I had to leave the house to collect my thoughts. I knew it was time to leave the marriage, but the fear of the unknown was trying to play a role in my decision. I was five months into a difficult pregnancy, and I was terrified of even the thought of raising two children alone. My marriage was emotionally bankrupt, and I knew my husband would always be connected to the mother of his first child. I felt like a failure, and it would be my second failed marriage. I didn't want him to go back to her and I didn't want her to feel like "she won," either, but I had to finally say enough is enough.

I continued to collect my thoughts as I drove around, and before I returned home, I decided to call my husband instead. He admitted his wrongdoing and it was just as I had suspected, he was still cheating on me to be with her. I became unglued and demanded he get out. I told him, by the time I arrived at home I wanted him GONE!!

Later that evening my girlfriend came over to console me and encouraged me to rest. Later that night when I did not feel the baby moving in my womb, I panicked. Thoughts of worry raced through my mind.

"What have I done?"

"Did I overreact?"

"I know I told him to get out, but how am I going to raise two children alone when I am already struggling?"

"What are my friends going to say?"

"Suppose 'she' finds out he is no longer with me?"

That night I'm sure I might have sent him more than a dozen text messages begging him to come back home. I called his phone back-to-back, pleading, but he never came home. Instead, he moved in with her.

I was familiar with God's presence. I felt his presence when I first found out I was pregnant with my husband's child. It felt like a warm blanket of love draping over me. I felt that same warm blanket of love come over me when I asked my husband to leave. That warm and loving experienced served as a reminder to me that I was not alone.

I was going to have to revisit the place of forgiveness because even though he was gone, my emotions were still imprisoned. My husband never apologized to me, and I continued to replay every heartache I experienced while connected to him. He had moved in with the mother of his first child and refused to sign the birth certificate of the child we created together. I did not want to waste my pain, so I knew forgiveness, which was the doorway to healing, was necessary. In my own strength, I knew I could not forgive him or her for the pain I endured, I needed Jesus to help me to forgive.

When I asked God to help me forgive, my forgiveness journey began with me forgiving myself. I asked God to teach me how to love myself and show me how to forgive myself. The more I forgave myself and began to love on myself, the easier life became. I became immersed in God's grace and was able to forgive others without an explanation, apology, or closure. Any time I felt a pinch of pain when his name was mentioned, or a song triggered a memory, or a scent reminded me of him, I immediately asked God to help me to forgive. I repeated that process as many times as I needed it and one day, I saw the fruit of forgiveness.

When it was time to sign the divorce papers, we appeared in domestic violence court and an emergency protective order was granted. My husband was granted the right to have supervised visits with our daughter, but after the third no-show for his scheduled visit, I later found out he had moved out of state and married the mother of his first child. The pain of that news was almost as painful as the time when he refused to sign our daughter's birth certificate. At that moment, I asked God to help me to surrender the disappointment and heartache to him and never take it back.

A year later, my then ex-husband returned with an apology. He told me how sorry he was for the way things unfolded. He acknowledged how terrible he treated me and told me how much he missed his family and wanted us back. In times past, he would ridicule me and be turned off by how easily I made myself available to him after his infidelity, but when he approached me that time, things were different. I was different. I was healed and I had forgiven him. I knew what love was and I knew who I was. I responded to him with confidence and kindness and told him he needed to learn how to love his wife. I know she did not honor our marriage, but I planted a seed by telling him to honor her by being faithful. I never felt loved or wanted in the relationship we had, and he admitted to never being faithful to me, however I had already forgiven him, and I wished him nothing but the best in his future. At the end of that conversation, I knew without any doubt I was healed, and I had truly forgiven him because there was no more pain. I didn't appreciate the way he approached me about getting back together, but I was grateful I was not the same woman he was once married to. I was healed. He was shocked by my response, but he had no other choice except to respect my firm NO. I had no intention or plans to go back to such a broken place. I was enjoying the freedom of living in the healing that only God could perform by transforming my heart.

I learned valuable lessons during that experience. I learned the value of seeing myself as God sees me and the value of receiving His love. My faith in Him pulled me through and transformed my heart and my mind. Had I not been willing to submit to His directions, I would not be the woman I am today. The more I surrendered to His direction and correction, the more I realized that my pain was not wasted. I returned to school to finish my bachelor's degree, which inspired me to move even further to pursue my master's in social work. Working with troubled teens, single mothers, and women that walked down the path of rejection, rebellion, and low self-esteem gives me life and I love to show them what hope looks and sounds like.

Going through that divorce felt like death, especially when my husband married the woman he cheated on me with. I could not see hope in that moment, but I'm grateful to God for helping me to overcome the pain and disappointment. Along the way, God helped me to help others. When I chose to submit to the truth, everything changed for me and my children. I am grateful that beauty came from those ashes and choosing to capitalize on the many lessons I learned has been instrumental in changing the trajectory of my life. As I continue to be a student and a mentor, serving and helping others, I am still very much an advocate for love and marriage. My pain was not wasted because at the end of the day, I found my voice. I recommitted my life to Christ and now I see myself as He sees me.

My life is committed to serving others from a place of victory because I have encountered the heartache and hardships of single parenthood and the trauma that divorce brings. I am operating from a place of forgiveness and wholeness when I declare to you that your life is not over. Keep living, learning, and loving!

**Three affirmations that helped me get through, and I hope they help you!**

1. I am loved.

2. I am valuable.

3. I am designed to receive and give love.

**Three questions I would like to ask you, to help you in your evolution!**

1. How do you see yourself? Read Ephesians 2:10

2. What have you compromised to obtain love? Read Romans 12:9

3. Are you wasting your pain? Read Deuteronomy 31:6

## REFLECTIONS FOR YOUR EVOLUTION

# No Regrets

## Kristan Bennerman

I woke up early and got dressed for work. I was looking forward to having an easy morning because I was headed to a meeting that was being held off-site. I loved the off-site meetings because I had an opportunity to spend a little time with my colleagues who I didn't get to see that often, and catch up on what's been going on. I met up with one of my co-workers and she drove us to the location.

Just as we were about to get started with the meeting, I glanced down at my phone and noticed I had received a text message from my husband's best friend. It was a bit strange for me to be getting a text message from him, especially so early in the morning. In his message, he asked me to call him, which set off a bit of an alarm on the inside of me, but I just kept myself calm. When I called him, he told me that he received a weird text message from my husband, and I could sense anxiety beginning to get the better of me. I knew something was wrong. I was the queen of the poker face and I rarely showed emotion in front of others, but I was clearly cracking. As I began to make my way to where my boss was standing, my knees almost buckled and as hard as I tried to contain my emotions, I was visibly shaken.

Without me saying a word, my boss saw the concern written all over my face. My voice was noticeably shaky when I told him I had to leave to check on my husband and, without hesitation, he told me to leave. My husband and I worked for the same company, so my boss knew who he was. My co-worker drove me back to my car and for the entire commute, I gently avoided her many questions or kept my answers short. My poker face persona remained intact during the drive to my car, and when we finally arrived at my car I calmly thanked her and got into my vehicle.

I drove home in what felt like slow motion. When I got out of the car and walked up to the house, I didn't even want to open the front door. I didn't know what to expect, so as I slowly entered and walked up the stairs, I was relieved when I heard the sound of my husband turning off the water in the shower. He was still alive! All of the anxiety I had carried throughout that morning took a brief exhale, but my husband shared with me a little later that he truly no longer wanted to live.

We spent the next several hours together while I tried to understand what had been going on in his mind to bring him to the point of entertaining suicidal thoughts. I tried to understand how and why I never knew he had battled suicidal thoughts for years.

That night, my husband had a breakdown and I had to decide whether or not I would have him admitted to a hospital. It was a hard decision, and even though he was not initially agreeable with the decision, he later realized it was ultimately the right call to make. The following morning, I packed his bag. I knew he was going to be hospitalized for at least a week, so as I was preparing his clothes I came across a folded piece of paper in his pocket.

At that point, we had been together for eight years. We met when I was in my last year of college and after I graduated we moved in together. Later we both relocated to Nashville from Kentucky, and from the very first moment I met his family, I was considered family. My family embraced him the same way. After we lived together for six years, we got married in a private and intimate ceremony surrounded by our loved ones. It felt perfect and removed any doubt I may have had before we said I do. The first six months of our marriage was what I would call marital bliss, but it slowly began to unravel. For almost a year, I lived in a state of confusion.

I never had a reason or a need to do any kind of detective work in our relationship, so when I came across that piece of folded piece of paper in his pocket, I simply unfolded it to see if it contained any important information. What I read stopped me in my tracks. It was a suicide note addressed to me, his family, and HER.

Now, this may sound a bit petty, but his family got a few words of him expressing his sorrow and I got a few words written to me, but *most* of the letter was written to HER expressing his love and gratitude. Now, how do you think I felt about finding that letter? Actually, I felt an enormous amount of relief. For a long time I was puzzled about why he was always willing to work so much overtime covering for his co-workers so they could attend their family activities, but was unwilling to take a day off for me. I was perplexed by the unanswered calls and the way he actively dismissed me in every way for months. It finally all made sense.

When I arrived at the hospital, my husband looked well-rested, peaceful, and didn't appear to resent me after the very rough night he had. He smiled when he saw me, and I smiled back at him, asking if there was anyone else he wished to be there. "No," was his response. I gave him a certain look and repeated my question.

"Is there anyone else you would prefer to be here at this time to help you? If so, let me know."

I continued to glare at him; and he knew exactly what I meant. He held firm to his response, so I stayed with him for a while. He was in the hospital for a few days and on the day I picked him up to return home, I let him know I would be willing to stay as long as I could to see him reach a better state of mind, but I assured him the marriage was over. I stayed because I remembered my vow to stay in sickness and in health, and I believed I could honor that vow.

I held a degree in social work, so I was familiar with mental illness. Close family members have suffered with depression and suicidal thoughts, which does not make a person weak. Mental illness is real. My experience has proven that some people process life differently, and it takes patience, love, and professional help, if needed, as a form of support. I didn't and don't take suicide lightly and if I can be a voice of reason, someone who listens, or be clear-headed enough to make decisions that will benefit a person in the future, I can be that person. As heroic as that may sound, I just stayed with him because I thought it was the right thing to do. Trust me, I was thinking about myself. I let it be known that the marriage was over. I said what I meant, and I meant what I said, so I quietly planned the process of my divorce.

Choosing to stay in the home we lived in together was an experience. Some days I was nice, some days I said nothing, and on other days I made small talk and listened. On his part, a lot of days he acted as if everything was normal. He expressed how he wanted to work on us and spend time with me. He wanted to explain to me, but I had nothing.

When I was younger, I remember hearing someone say, "When a man cheats, it's usually not because he wants to leave; and I also heard the saying "When a woman is done, she is done." I found both of those statements to be true. I spent months asking him if everything was okay, asking him to talk to me; to spend a few hours with me, or to plan a vacation. Well, I no longer wanted to talk about anything. I had no questions for him, and I required no explanations. I was done.

During that time, my husband and I worked for the same company, but in different buildings. I usually kept to myself and paid attention to my own business, so if something was wrong with me, it wasn't something I let anybody and everybody know about. Remember? I was the queen of the poker face. I had never in my life been surrounded by so much drama; where everyone knows my personal business. Knowing that they were talking behind my back, I sucked it up, ignored it, and threw myself into work. I began to navigate my career so that I could position myself to be financially secure whenever I was ready to make the transition. Giving more focus to my fitness routine also helped me to connect more with God. I often asked him to make everything better or continue to strengthen me so my mom would not have to worry about me. The last leg of my process involved me looking for my own place. I moved to a smaller place in Nashville, and my husband moved back home to Kentucky. I was not ready to move back to Kentucky because, after all, I was already established in Nashville. I wasn't going to allow his poor decision to push me back home to Kentucky.

When the movie Waiting to Exhale came out, I could not fully relate to it because I was too young and hadn't experienced life and relationships up to that point. However, there was one infamous scene I will never forget. Bernadine smoked a cigarette with her back facing the car, full of her cheating husband's belongings which she had just set on fire. As an adult, I could relate and it all made sense. I felt that as a teen and I certainly felt it as an adult. That was my favorite scene, but I didn't want to move forward as a bitter black woman, or even a bitter woman. I chose not to be bitter, but to be positive and have a positive influence in my new life.

In order to move forward unhindered, I needed to heal completely. My healing process began when I took a look at what I did wrong and made a commitment to myself to do better the next time. When my husband and I had dated for six years. When I moved to Nashville with him, I didn't want to just continue to live with him, I wanted to be married to him, but he never moved fast enough for me. He wasn't the type who made things happen, he just dealt with things when they happened. There was no sense of measurement of how far or how close he was from achieving the goal. Eventually, I gave him an ultimatum. Either we got married or it was over. Nothing about that was romantic. I always tell people to not take my choice away from me or make a decision for me, but isn't that what I did for him?

I had to take some accountability for our relationship in order to heal. In our relationship, I controlled our money and bills at his request because he didn't like dealing with it. He didn't like making decisions or even discussing issues. I was the decision-maker. On his days off, he played video games. On my days off, I cleaned, and on the days I worked, I cleaned. Trust me, I let him know about it too. In the end, I realized constantly telling someone what you need and how you need it to be done, does not necessarily make them want do it if they don't want to do it. I was calling out for a team player, but all he heard was he couldn't do anything right.

Forgiving myself was a crucial element of my healing, but I also had to forgive others. I forgave my ex-husband because I understood how life gets in the way and people make mistakes. He made a mistake. It was hard to let go of a family that was once mine, but I felt good knowing he was in good hands because he deserves to be happy. When I had to chase him down for months to sign the divorce papers, resentment tried to creep in again, but once he signed them, I forgave him again and have been able to move on.

As far as forgiving the other woman, I never gave her much thought outside of gathering the information I needed to know about the affair. She did not stand before God and our families promising to be faithful to me, but he did.

That experience helped me to see how vital a good support system full of family, close friends, and married friends is. It was years later before I even told my mom everything that had happened. I didn't share my struggle with her while I was going through it in Nashville because I didn't want her to feel sorry for me or worry about me. My nature had always been to fix the problem first, then tell the story.

When I finally moved back to Kentucky for family reasons, I never planned to date again but I found myself in the dating age of cell phones, text messages, social media, and various dating sites. I learned everyone was dating everyone, had way too much access, and everything was a game. I couldn't handle that because I am who I say I am and if you ask me a question, I will honestly answer anything about myself. I didn't see that same quality in anyone I dated.

I finally put to rest the resentment I was holding onto because my ex-husband had not given me any children and I became content in knowing I didn't have to be married or have children to be happy. I stayed in Kentucky for more six years and decided I would still put my best foot forward in the dating game. I realigned my goals and found other things that made me feel whole, and for a while dating just wasn't something I wanted to do.

I usually don't take relationship advice from Steve Harvey, but I agreed with a statement he once made. He said there is no need to search for a good man because a good man will find you. The hunt is over when he finds the one. Well, on a trip to visit friends in Nashville, he found me.

He was the one who God sent to be my husband and one morning, while overlooking the Nashville skyline, he got down on one knee and asked me to marry him. Maybe one day we will have a child together, but my husband has already given me an amazing bonus son. Years ago, I heard a wise person say "Marry someone you can't live without." I saw that as more of a figure of speech because there were a lot of people who I could say I could live without. However, today, there is one person I could not imagine living a day without -- Christian Bennerman.

I used to question why any woman would stay when their husband cheated on them, but I learned during the demise of my marriage to never judge others. I now understand why a person would stay in their marriage. Yes, if you can put in the work necessary to save your marriage, do it. Marriage isn't without flaws, but it can be beautiful. I said I do in front of God and my family and I never saw anyone in my family divorce. Everyone was married with kids in their early twenties and stayed no matter what happened. In the end, I had to let that go. God loves me and would never want me to be unhappy. Although some of my family might have never seen that coming from me, the responsible one, they have never allowed me to believe they would love me less and welcomed me home with open arms.

Sometimes it's hard to vocalize what we like about ourselves, but I wake up every day and proudly look at myself in the mirror. Loving and respecting myself in a way that works for me is a decision I have made, and although I realize no one is perfect, I still actively apply the life lessons I have learned and incorporate them into my current marriage. I will be forever grateful for the second chance to love again. If it can be said that "even on my best day I don't deserve anything," I can't emphasize enough how thankful I am to have been blessed to have the most amazing husband in the world.

**Three affirmations that helped me get through, and I hope they help you!**

1. I may have my moments, but quitting is not an option.
2. I wake up in the morning grateful that God has given me another day.
3. I can do it alone, but I'm overjoyed that I don't have to.

**Three questions I would like to ask you to help you in your evolution!**

1. Using my story of suicide as an example, how would you have reacted?
2. I chose to leave my marriage. Would you have left? Why or why not?
3. How might your religious beliefs play into your past, present, and future relationships?

## REFLECTIONS FOR YOUR EVOLUTION

# About The Authors

## *Patrice Bush Visionary Author*

Patrice Bush is the Founder and CEO of It Takes 2 Marriage Coaching, where Wedding VOWS turn into Wedding WOWS. It Takes 2 Marriage Coaching helps to strengthen families through Couples Coaching, Destination Marriage Retreats, Workshops, Support Groups and Speaking Engagements. It Takes 2, has served over 3000 couples from across 38 U.S. States. From 2014 – 2016 Patrice lead the dynamic radio show, *Marriage Matters*, with over eight thousand listeners. Patrice is a powerful speaker using from both academic and personal experience on relationships. Patrice is the author of Celebrate Our Love Couple's Journal, Repairing Your Christian Marriage: Faith Based Strategies to Rebuild Your Relationship, Evolve: From Heart Breaks to Hearts Healed and Evolve Vol. II: Recovering The Woman Within The Love is Over Not You. She has appeared on FOX news, Wake Up Charlotte and several radio shows across the country and she has been published in the Charlotte Parent magazine.

## About The Authors

Patrice has hosted 41 Destination Marriage Retreats and over 100 local & national events for couples and families.

## Popular Speaking Topics

- The Superwoman Complex: But WHO is Going To Save YOU?
- Divorce Proof: 10 Practical Strategies To a Save Your Marriage From Divorce
- Love & Commitment; The Difference Between The Two
- My Children, Your Children: Mastering Blending Families
- Entrepreneur Hang ups, Fall Outs & Raising To Success
- Love Languages
- Meshing Communication Styles

**For more information:**

www.ItTakes2MarriageCoaching.com

www.PatriceBush.com

admin@ItTakes2MarriageCoaching.com

704-449-6542

## *Nichelle Nelson*

Ms. Nichelle Nelson is the CEO and Founder of Flawlessly Flawed which is an Empowerment Initiative to Heal with Love through LIVING. It also serves as the parent company that manages Designs by N2 IINC., Kreativ Concept Mgmt., and Flawlessly Flawed Media. She has over 30 plus years of experience in the Fashion & Entertainment Industry to include Assistant Editor for I-Fashion Magazine of New York, Assistant Director of Carolina Girls Rock Pageant, and a Motivational Speaker on the Faith Over Fear Tour. She is a former Professional Model, Fashion Show Producer, and Runway Choreographer to name a few. As a Motivational speaker, she is sharing her journey and life lessons that brought her closer to GOD. She has a passion for empowering young girls and women and instilling in them that there is nothing they can't achieve through faith and the courage they have inside to be successful in life. She is also an advocate for women who have been mistreated, abused, and cheated on in marriage. Ms. Nelson has always been an aspiring writer. Her passion for literature and romance novels took her on journeys that could only be found on the pages of her favorite authors. Nichelle is mostly proud of her number one role as MOM to 3 boys; Tywon (33), Jabari (27), and Tyler (12), and Glam Ma to her beautiful grandchildren. She currently resides in Mooresville, NC on Lake Norman and is a member of Inheritance Church of Christ.

Instagram: nichelle_nelson

Facebook: Nichelle Nelson

### Suan-Nesha Fuller Scott

Suan-Nesha Fuller Scott lives in Charlotte, NC. She has a Master of Science in Nursing Degree. She has over 23 years of nursing experience working with children and families. She is a Certified Case Manager and has spent the past two years working in Case management with children and adults in a community-based clinic. Suan-Nesha loves reading, dancing, and spending time with family. She is grateful for the love, support, and encouragement of her sisters, niece, and extended family members. She would like to dedicate her literary work to the memory of her late mother Emma Fuller and her late mother-in-law Helen Scott.

Suan-Nesha is a mother of one biological son and one bonus son. Her bonus son is grown, married and in the armed forces and her baby boy is 4 years old.

*About The Authors*

## *J. Tyneka Nelson*

J. Tyneka Nelson is a phenomenal spiritual force to be reckoned with. At the tender age of eight, Tyneka became a published author. Her very first poem was featured in the book entitled The Silent Word. Tyneka is also the CEO of The Jazmeen Miles Anencephaly Foundation: a non-profit in honor of her daughter Jazmeen, that has transitioned to Heaven. The Founder of A Moment In Time Event Planning LLC, Nelson and Moore Ventures LLC, and J. J. and T. Travel Management Group, Tyneka still has a professional career as the Vice President of a Fortune 500 company, where she has proudly worked for the past 18 years. Tyneka has discovered that the ocean is therapy for her, as she does her best writing and emotional and mental processing through the ocean. She desires to encourage and motivate others by sharing personal life experiences. The amount of love shown, the advice given, and the resources she shares demonstrate her desire daily. One of Tyneka's life philosophies is "if my pain, loss, or heartache helps at least one person to realize they can make it through their storm, then it was worth it."

Tyneka is a wonderful wife to Kirk and very involved mother of three daughters: Jaleah is fourteen years old, Jazmeen would have been eight years old (Heaven), and Kyra is three years old.

*About The Authors*

## *Venus J. Jackson*

Venus J. Jackson decided to make Rock Hill, South Carolina home after receiving her Bachelor of Arts degree from Winthrop University twenty-five years ago. She has since gone on to receive two additional degrees including her Master of Arts in Human Resource Management from Webster University. Currently, Ms. Jackson works as a dedicated Human Resource Coordinator, doing what she loves, helping people. Venus enjoys the many organizations of which she is a part of, her church family, giving back to her community, writing poetry, and of course reading and listening to a terrific audiobook. Ms. Jackson has had her inspiring poetry for mother's experiencing the loss of a child cited in the Empty Arms national organization's publication. Now, the journey to become fully healed following the ending of her sixteen-year marriage is what Ms. Jackson desires to share in hopes to help another person who may feel that they are or were also drowning in their marriage. Her selfless desire to inspire another person's journey from heartbreak to heart-healed is both as commendable and as encouraging as her journey itself.

She is a devoted mother of three to a set of adult twin daughters and a twelve-year-old son.

*About The Authors*

## Kerrie L. Brittingham

Kerrie L. Brittingham received her undergraduate degree in Psychology from Kentucky Wesleyan College in 1997 and her master's in social work from Spaulding University in 2005. Kerrie is a licensed clinical Social Worker in the State of Kentucky and has 15 years of experience providing therapy to children and families. She provided therapy at a residential treatment facility for children that have been removed from their birth homes, she also provided family therapy to help reunite children and families when appropriate. She also worked with children that needed to be placed in foster or adoptive homes. She worked with children in other capacities for an additional five years. She also completed the two-year Conjoint Marital and Family Counseling Program and is trained in providing Parent-Child Interaction Therapy. Kerrie completed the Juvenile Sex Offender Counselor certification program through the Kent School of Social Work. She now owns her own private practice and provides therapy for children, teens, adults, couples, and families. Aside from being a professional, Kerrie is a mother of two very busy teenagers!

## Dwan Warren

Dwan Warren was born and raised outside the city of Frankfort, in the beautiful bluegrass state of Kentucky. Dwan considers her faith and family to be most important to her. If she is not spending time with her friends and family, you can always find her creating beautiful trendy bows at Hannah's Garden of Bows and doing outreach with her bandmates by rocking it out as At His Feet. *Evolve II Recovering the Woman Within; The Love is Over Not You* is Dwan's first book.

Dwan Warren paints a picture of a person who perseveres through heartache and hardship. While sharing the lessons regarding the power of faith, the value of identity, and the liberation in forgiveness.

## *Kristan Bennerman*

Kristan Bennerman is from Somerset, KY and currently lives in Nashville, TN. She obtained her Bachelors of Art in Social Work and recently finished her MBA with a focus in Healthcare Administration. For more than fifteen years she has worked in management and banking. Today, she continues her education in Nursing. Nursing will open many doors for her in healthcare, but she is most excited about bringing her expertise to her husband's oral surgery practice. With her experience she will add laser and botox to his already booming business. Together they are a team.

Kristan is passionate about health. Lifting weights, running on the treadmill, and stair master is how she releases the day. She loves hiking, yoga, and spin classes. She has always enjoyed reading and has her own stories to tell.

Kristan has been happily married for one year and counting. She and her husband enjoy everything from popcorn and movie nights on the couch to travelling to new places. Through marriage she has been blessed with a bonus son. He is a rising basketball star. During the winter you can find Kristan's family in the

*About The Authors*

bleachers and travelling to various AAU games during the Spring and Summer. They all love spoiling their new goldendoodle named Mocha.

www.ingramcontent.com/pod-product-compliance
Lightning Source LLC
Chambersburg PA
CBHW072038110526
44592CB00012B/1475